THE
LLADRÓ®
GUIDE

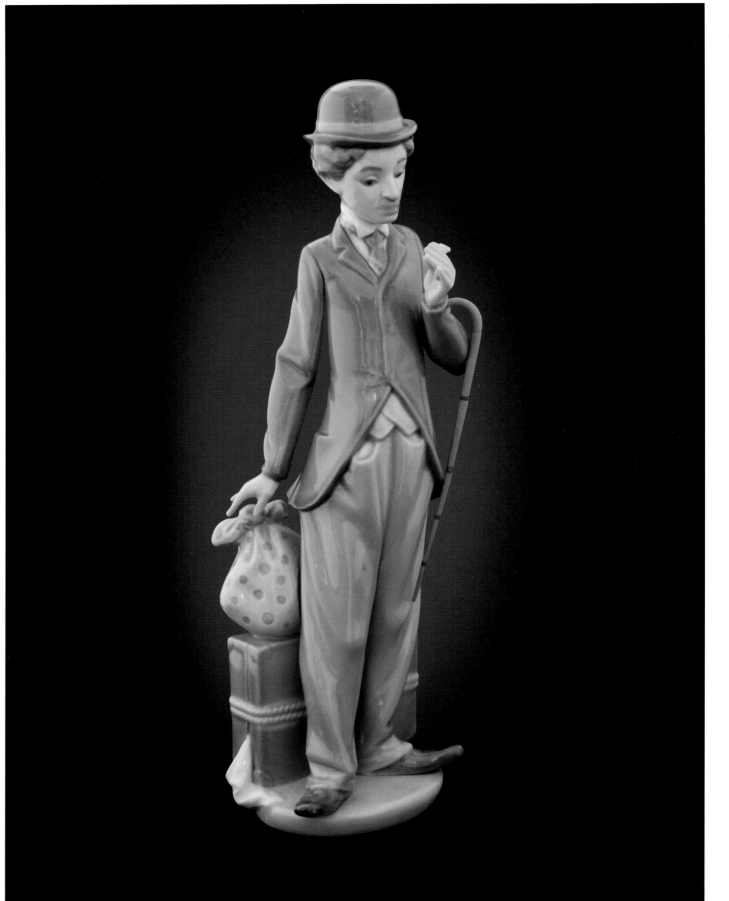

THE LLADRÓ® GUIDE

A Collector's Reference to Retired Porcelain Figurines in Lladró Brands

PEGGY ROSE WHITENECK

SCHIFFER
PUBLISHING

4880 Lower Valley Road · Atglen, PA 19310

This book is dedicated to
Janet Gale Hammer,
whose friendship and enthusiasm for Lladró
have sustained me in countless ways,
and
in loving memory of my parents, Patricia
Ann Armstrong Whiteneck & George Harold
Whiteneck, who taught me a love for
beautiful things.

Designed by Danielle D. Farmer
Cover design by Brenda McCallum
Except as otherwise indicated in the captions, photos in the book are by the author from her own collection.
Type set in Amerigo BT/Helvetica Narrow

ISBN: 978-0-7643-5839-5
Printed in China

Published by Schiffer Publishing, Ltd.
4880 Lower Valley Road
Atglen, PA 19310
Phone: (610) 593-1777; Fax: (610) 593-2002
E-mail: Info@schifferbooks.com
Web: www.schifferbooks.com

For our complete selection of fine books on this and related subjects, please visit our website at www.schifferbooks.com. You may also write for a free catalog.

Schiffer Publishing's titles are available at special discounts for bulk purchases for sales promotions or premiums. Special editions, including personalized covers, corporate imprints, and excerpts, can be created in large quantities for special needs. For more information, contact the publisher.

We are always looking for people to write books on new and related subjects. If you have an idea for a book, please contact us at proposals@schifferbooks.com.

CONTENTS

One of the reasons Lladró has been so successful is the technical risks the company takes with the porcelain medium, constantly pushing the limits to see how far the material can be stretched.

ACKNOWLEDGMENTS

The illustrations in this book are truly an international effort! I am most grateful to Janet Gale Hammer and to collectors Brad Welch in the US, Teresa K. Schmitt in the US, Jorge L. Gonzalez Rodriguez in the United Kingdom, Joëlle Ley in Belgium, and Carlos D. Zepeda Abrego in El Salvador for their photo contributions to this book.

INTRODUCTION

Although Lladró makes many other kinds and shapes of decorative porcelain (including vases, picture frames, centerpieces, lamps, and so on), it is best known for its figurines, the area of greatest collector interest. Consequently, this is a book that focuses on retired figurine models in Lladró's several brands.

"Dog with Snail," also made without the snail. Both have old, pre-logo-impressed marks and escaped capture in the belated cataloging dragnet Lladró cast in the late '70s and early '80s in order to reconstruct its production history. A third variant is known with a bone in the dog's mouth. $350–$400.

Ironically, retired models that are no longer in production are also the area of greatest new discovery. Hardly a week goes by that I'm not contacted via email by a collector, somewhere in the world, who has found a previously unknown yet certifiably genuine model in one of the Lladró brands. Part of the fun of being a Lladró collector today is this continual discovery of formerly unknown models.

WHY LLADRÓ?

There are many reasons that even people of means, who have many options for the disposition of their discretionary income, would choose to spend some of it on Lladró. In the first place, Lladró models (with the exception of one obscure brand called Hispania, an acquired ceramic company no longer in production) are made of fine porcelain, historically considered one of the world's most precious materials. Fine porcelain has always been expensive and always treasured.

One of the reasons Lladró has been so successful is the technical risks the company takes with the porcelain medium, constantly pushing the limits to see how far the material can be stretched. The interesting way in which its models occupy space is one of Lladró's distinguishing features that set it apart from its contemporary competitors in Spain and elsewhere in the world. Lladró models have a kind of animation about them; when one looks at a Lladró figurine, one almost expects it to get up and move off its shelf. Creating this dynamism takes peerless technical and artistic skill.

Lladró models also have a distinctive aesthetic delicacy, particularly in facial features, which I have found to be the one inimitable and most telling clue, other than a genuine brand mark, to Lladró authenticity. Lladró faces are delicately modeled and painted. One doesn't see on Lladró the coarsely applied black eye features (in eyebrows, for example) that are typical in the work of competitors trying unsuccessfully to imitate its style. While Lladró works in ethnically and racially diverse themes, it adopts the same subtle approach to all, an approach that both respects the dignity of our common humanity *and* the dignity of particular cultures, suggesting distinctive ethnic facial features without stereotyping or caricaturing them.

The modeling detail in a Lladró brand figurine is exquisite; one can see the weaving in a basket, the yarn strands in a knit afghan, the trim on a dress hem, the muscle definition in a dog. In human models, hands and even fingers are separately and delicately articulated. As art itself is a window on the world, teaching us to see when we look, so Lladró invites us into its vision of the world and bids us to appreciate the divine in the details.

My own attraction to the delicacy and detailing in Lladró porcelain has led me in turn to other porcelain enthusiasms, including various types of Asian antique porcelains. In this sense, Lladró has opened me to an entire world of porcelain with its centuries of tradition that I might otherwise not have known.

WHY THIS BOOK?

Since the early decades of Lladró's rise to international popularity over more than a half century, there has been an intense—one might even say insatiable— collector demand for information about it. This demand has not been satisfied by the several limited-circulation books formerly put out by the company itself, nor by my own first books on Lladró (now out of print), nor by the several websites devoted to Lladró. Just as the tactility of porcelain is a significant part of its allure, so collectors seem to want reference books they can hold in their hands and not just read on a screen.

There has also been a keen interest in Lladró's other and affiliated brands (most notably NAO, Rosal, Zaphir, and Golden Memories), about which there is little information available to collectors, in part because of the manufacturer's reluctance (for marketing reasons explored in this book) to publish information about its alternate brands. Moreover, collectors are curious about brand crossover, in which some early models were made under more than one Lladró brand name. Far from diminishing collector interest, discovery of this "brand cloning" appears to have intensified interest by increasing the availability of certain early models formerly thought to be impossible to acquire on the secondary market. At the same time, the presence of unique models in each of the brands has greatly expanded Lladró collecting potential. Taken together, these factors have led many serious Lladró collectors to enthusiastically diversify their "regular" Lladró collections with the best of Lladró's other brands.

As a further intriguing challenge in model identification, some individual and identical models have been found with not just two but as many as three different Lladró brand marks! For instance, individual examples of the little Cocker without snail shown in this introduction have been found marked either Lladró, NAO, or Rosal. (I should add here that any claims in this book for multiple brand production of the same model are made after I have seen the evidence myself.)

"Flying Herons (a.k.a. "Cranes"), early NAO model #44, issued some time in the mid- to late 1960s, was retired in its matte version in 1991 and glazed in 2001. Extremely delicate necks, heads, and beaks extend into space in a way that is inimitable for competing companies in Valencia. $150–$200.

"Faces will always tell." Note the careful modeling detail in this little girl's face ("Girl with Lamb," #1010 M). In a Lladró, the forehead, eye orbits, cheek structure, nose, lips, and chin will be well and carefully articulated, even in profile.

First issued in 1973, the matte version of "DEATH OF THE SWAN" (#4855), shown here, was retired in 1991, the glazed version not until 2000. A fine example both of the beauty of Lladró and the risks Lladró sculptors take in the ways their models occupy space. Sculptor: Vicente Martinez. $400–$450.

Like nature itself, collectors abhor a vacuum. Deprived of access to facts about Lladró brand diversification, collectors may too readily allow rumor and invention to fill the gap. The most infamous and persistent of these apocryphal legends is that one of the Lladró brothers (or an uncle, cousin, or some other relative, depending on the version) "turned renegade" and struck out from the others to start his own company. Although untrue, the rumor has legs that have taken it all over the world, and it is given a kind of perpetual zombie life through repetition in online auctions that cannibalize one another for their item descriptions. In part, then, this book is intended as a corrective for such misinformation.

The book is not, however, intended as a comprehensive catalog of everything Lladró ever made. Those looking for comprehensive catalogs and specific model identification are referred to the web catalogs already set up for this purpose: the official Lladró website (www.lladro.com) and Janet Hammer's A Retired Collection (www.aretiredcollection.com) for the regular/core Lladró collection; the official NAO website (www.naoporcelain.com); and, for the NAO, Zaphir, and Golden Memories brands, my own collector information website, El Portal Porcelana (www.elportalporcelana.info).

WHY THIS AUTHOR?

Early on, the Lladró company had not foreseen the stunning global success of what began as a small, family-owned entrepreneurial venture. Consequently, the company hadn't initially focused on record keeping for posterity, and there are many holes in its early production records. The company found itself, by the early 1980s, in a scramble to try to respond to collectors clamoring for information on older models.

Lladró's branch in the US was initially charged with overseeing this information reconstruction, with results published in the company's *Lladró Authorized Reference Guide*, the first edition of which came out in 1981 and the last

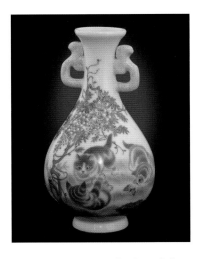

My experience as a Lladró collector led me to the delicate and finely detailed painting on better Asian porcelains such as this Chinese vase, purchased at an antique shop. The blossoms are exquisitely applied with enamel paint, the kittens with whisker-thin brushstrokes to delineate fur.

I have two identical versions of "Hunting Dog," one with a NAO-impressed mark and the other with a Lladró-impressed mark (model number 308.13 in the regular Lladró collection and made in 1963). Sculptor: Fulgencio García. $700–$750 (either mark).

"Ostrich Group" with impressed NAO mark (NAO #46). An identical model has also been found with an old, impressed Lladró mark (model #297.13), both created by the same sculptor and the same company and made in the same time period (early to mid-1960s). Sculptor: Fulgencio García. $750–$850 (either mark).

Juan Huerta's endearing portrait of a curious boy watching the shy hand-wringing of a little girl in "Boy Meets Girl" (#1188 G/M), retired in 1989. It was first issued in 1972, so versions from the 1970s will not have the serial number on the base. Sculptor: Juan Huerta. $300–$350.

edition in 2006, and in its four-volume *Lladró Encyclopedia*, which covers production through 1996. The effort relied, to a great extent, on the memories, experiences, and model evidence supplied by veteran collectors. On the basis of available records, the *Guide* had identified certain models with Lladró marks, those it cataloged with decimal point serial numbers, as being "very rare"—practically prototypic—because company reps quite literally did not *know* there were other Lladró brands, much less that several of the decimal-numbered rarities were actually issued in one or more of those brands.

Meanwhile, Lladró collecting was so segmented (in part as a company marketing policy) that collectors of one Lladró brand simply didn't talk to collectors of another. As a collector myself, I had a boundless curiosity about the many items I saw on the secondary market that I recognized as Lladró even though they weren't marked as such. I also had other Lladró questions to which Lladró company customer service reps could not provide answers. Fortunately, I very much enjoy doing research. Consequently, I can claim, in all humility, to be one of the few people with a sufficiently comprehensive familiarity with all the Lladró brands, gathered over years of research and experience, to be able to write coherently about the relationships between them.

Throughout those years of research, I've used a variety of evidence sources: actual models and model comparisons in the various Lladró brands, brand marks and their relative ages and evolution, books produced by the company itself, old company retail catalogs, information from company representatives, the experience of veteran collectors, etc. These sources, even those from the company itself, often conflicted with one another. In reconciling these accounts, I've had to factor in the inherent plasticity of human memory; events and chronology are not necessarily remembered in all particulars as they actually occurred, resulting in oral and written accounts that are at odds not only with one another but, at times, even with model evidence.

Where interpretations of the evidence presented in this book differ, I will say so. Whatever of my own interpretations and reconciliations of conflicting information are presented here are also flagged as such and, if not absolutely verifiable, are meant to be at least consistent with and plausible in light of the known facts.

ABOUT MODEL NUMBERS

Model numbers in this book are those assigned by the Lladró company and, in the case of Lladró's core brand and models that originated in NAO, Golden Memories, and Hispania, are unique to each brand. Zaphir models initially also had a unique set of numbers. However, when the Zaphir brand was discontinued and its models then in production were taken over into the NAO brand, the Zaphir model numbers for those items were retained in NAO.

This book uses the original model-numbering system followed by the letters *G* or *M*, in which *G* stands for a glazed finish, and *M* stands for matte (unglazed). A model number followed by *G/M* means the model was made in both forms. When an item is not followed by one of these letters, it means the item was made of a special ceramic formula where those letters do not apply—for example, the 2000- and 3000-series numbers in the regular Lladró line that are assigned to Gres models (a term explained later in this book) and the 100-series numbers assigned to a similar treatment in the Zaphir brand.

The Lladró company has more recently adopted a numbering system consisting of zeros and ones as a prefix to the model number to distinguish glazed from matte, but I find this system cumbersome and visually confusing. For purposes of this book, I have opted to stick with the old letter suffixes. It should also be noted that Lladró began stamping the four-digit model number into the base of its figurines only in the mid-1980s, so older retired models will not have model numbers on their base.

ABOUT THE ESTIMATED VALUES IN THIS BOOK

I've conceived of this project as a collector information book in the broader sense and not primarily a price guide. At the same time, I find that collector information books that sidestep entirely the matter of price are not very satisfying for readers. Consequently, I have included, with very few exceptions, either the last retail price on recently retired items as the benchmark for value, or a relatively conservative value price range for each of the items pictured in the book. All value numbers in the book are in USD (US dollars). These estimated price ranges aim for a balance between unrealistically high and unnecessarily low prices. Their purpose is not to direct or control the market. Collectors may be able to find, in shops or online, items in this book at well below my suggested values, and also prices well above.

This is a book primarily for collectors passionate about Lladró porcelains. For such collectors, resale value is not the first thing they think about when they find a retired Lladró on the secondary market—and this is what distinguishes a collector from a casual consumer or someone "decorating to impress" or someone buying speculatively for resale. For collectors, the ups and downs in the collectibles market matter less than the inherent attraction of a beautiful object. Having said that, no one likes to see the value of a collection decrease, and it must be admitted that prices for collectibles generally, including Lladró, took a substantial hit during the post-9/11 recessionary period and have never fully recovered to the overheated levels of the 1990s.

Lladró's "Little Friends" (#6129 G), made 1994–98 at a last retail price of $235. The longer this model is out of production, the less likelihood of finding a pristine example without breakage in one or more of the birds, enhancing the value of pristine examples. Sculptor: Joan Coderch. $300–$325.

When someone asks what a given antique or collectible is worth, there are several ways to answer the question because there are several meanings of the term "value" when it comes to antiques and collectibles:

Insurance replacement value: What someone would have to pay to replace an insured item more or less immediately after the loss and from a source known to have it. This tends to be on the high side for retired Lladró items, particularly the older models that aren't readily available for price shopping.[1]

Book value: Suggested values in published price guides and collector books, which tend to be either highly optimistic or pessimistically low, depending on how much the author him/herself knows about and values the particular collectible and on how the author is feeling about the market in any given year.

Fair market value (a.k.a. resale value): What a private seller could expect to get for or have to pay for a given item on the "open market." This value tends to be on the low side for retired collectibles that are fairly commonly available, resulting in the so-called buyer's market in price competition.

This set of "Penguins" (*left to right*, model #s 5249, 5248, and 5247 G) had a short retail run (1984–88) at last retail price of $85 each. I bought them in 1997 from A Retired Collection for $200 apiece. Sculptor: Fulgencio García. $250–$300 ea.

Collector value: A term of my own invention, based less on what's going on generally in the collectibles marketplace and more on the intangibles of collecting, such as aesthetics and technical quality. Collectors will often be willing to pay a price premium for these intangibles.

We must also admit that eBay™ has had a dampening effect on the value of antiques and collectibles by vastly increasing supply, especially on less expensive items, to the point where it outstrips demand. No longer are consumers dependent on locally available acquisition in the Lladró company's tightly controlled and restricted retail distribution network; eBay™ and other online sales sites provide a global marketplace with exponentially more opportunities to buy what have become, through the miracle of electronic commerce, commonly available items. The exception is genuinely rare Lladró, which continues to garner high prices because such items simply aren't generally available—not even on eBay™. On the other hand, eBay™ has sometimes served to provide needed relativity for the term "rare" by flushing out, after some seller's big "score" on a scarce Lladró, surprising quantities of that same model pulled from storage places around the world.

Still, I do not accept the notion, sometimes advanced by amateur appraisers and the media, that eBay™ sets "fair market value." For all its clout, eBay™ is just one sales and purchase venue in the wider marketplace of antiques and collectibles. Serious collectors will often pay a premium for convenience and the ability to examine an item directly and in real time before buying, even if they "could get it cheaper on eBay." Moreover, Lladró collectors will often pay a considerable premium over eBay™ prices in order to get a scarce item from a respected secondary-market Lladró broker who can guarantee the item's authenticity, condition, and provenance. It must also be acknowledged that how well a Lladró model does on eBay™, relative to other examples of its kind in the same venue, depends on many factors unrelated to the object itself, such as timing of the auction, whether or not the item has a reserve, the seller's reputation in eBay's publicly visible customer feedback system, and so on.

With all that in mind, collectors should understand the estimated value ranges given for individual items in this book as just that (estimates), and that values may fluctuate according to factors such as changes in item availability on the secondary market. Ultimately, the answer to the question "What's it worth?" is "Whatever you (or another collector) would pay for it." That figure may be either considerably less than the heart's desire of a seller—or, on the other hand, surprisingly high for a buyer willing to compete for a desired item at auction.

IN SPANISH PORCELAIN, THERE'S LLADRÓ AND THEN THERE ARE THE REST

There are many very small porcelain manufactories working in and around the Valencia region of Spain. They have limited name recognition, have no export beyond Spain (making their way outside that country via tourist suitcases), and, with few exceptions, do not have websites. They do not publish retail or collector catalogs. Consequently, it is impossible to identify individual models produced by these companies. And as many frustrated owners of these wannabe models have discovered, it's just no fun to collect things about which there is no available information and, consequently, no market demand.

More importantly, most of these competitor companies work "in the Lladró style" but produce models that are inferior to Lladró both technically and aesthetically. As collectors become more experienced and sophisticated, they learn to readily distinguish these from Lladró brands. I'm confident that I've developed a reasonable enough familiarity with all known Lladró brands that novice collectors may safely assume that if the brand name isn't in this book, it isn't a Lladró product.

CHAPTER 1

THE MAKING OF LLADRÓ

The Lladró brothers—Juan, José, and Vicente, in birth order from eldest to youngest—were brought up on and helped work a family farm in the Valencia region of Spain in the 1930s and early 1940s.

The most illuminating source for the early history of their somewhat unlikely venture into fine porcelain production is middle brother José Lladró's memoir, *Passenger of Life: Memories and Opinions of an Entrepreneur,* published in 2002. José reveals that it was actually the boys' mother who supplied the initial ambition that propelled her sons into some other line of work beyond the subsistence farming that had been their father's lot.

But if their mother wasn't interested in seeing her sons grow up to be poor farmers, she had no interest, either, in seeing them spend their lives as struggling artists. Although her vision for them probably didn't extend to their forming their own company, she certainly saw involvement in the burgeoning Valencian ceramics industry as their route to a decent livelihood.

Judging from photographs of the brothers' early works, José Lladró may have been the most artistically talented of the three. However, his mother's "business first" philosophy made an especially strong impression on this middle son, by some accounts the business acumen behind the company,[1] who wrote in his memoir, "I do not want to fool anyone: at first it was not genuine artistic interest, but instead my intuition that told me that by developing this [artistic] capability a road would be opened up before me that would lead me out of poverty."[2]

"Some accounts" apparently included their mother's. According to José's memoir, Mama Lladró extracted an oft-repeated promise from José's wife, Carmen, that Carmen would take it upon herself to make sure the three brothers did not split up and go their separate business ways. Evidence suggests their mother was so keen on this point because she believed her middle son's talents were somehow the glue that would hold together the family fortunes. In a poem written by Carmen to José and printed in his memoir, Carmen quotes her mother-in-law: "*Carmen, Carmen, promise me you will never let Pepe* [José's family nickname] *fly alone, because alone very high he will fly, but have him take care of the others because Pepe will make everyone fly.*"[3] The mother's determination that her sons remain together in business was decisive for at least the first fifty years or so of the Lladró company's history, and such a strong maternal influence would have been unusual in a patriarchal culture such as that in Spain.

It's fun to wonder whether the teenaged Lladró brothers might have been involved in making this old Nalda model. Painting is a bit primitive (the flowers on the skirt may be a stencil), but details such as the apples and weaving in the basket may foreshadow later Lladró.

After their graduation from the Valencian School of Arts and Crafts, the young brothers began their ceramics career working for at least two other companies, a tile factory and another ceramics company called Nalda. (The latter is still in business and is devoted these days to industrial-porcelain applications such as electrical insulators; however, during a very brief foray, sometime around the late 1940s, when the brothers worked there, it also produced porcelain figurines.) The management of both companies was threatened by the artistic and entre-preneurial energies of the sibling threesome, who had begun their own ceramic experiments with a succession of backyard kilns. More to the point, the young men had begun marketing their own products in competition with their employ-ers. In both instances, when given the ultimatum to cease and desist from com-petition or leave the employ, the brothers—fortunately for Lladró collectors—chose to strike out on their own.

THE MAKING OF A COMPANY

The Lladrós started their own business with a couple of very early collaborators, one of whom was sculptor Fulgencio García, a seminally important figure in the history of the company and one who would feature prominently in the evolution of Lladró's other brands (about which, more in subsequent chapters of this book). The Lladrós' first small retail shop opened in the early 1950s and carried not only their own work, but also gift wares purchased from other companies, including Hispania Ceramics (see chapter 6), a manufactory the brothers would eventually buy some decades later.[4]

In these early years, the Lladró company was literally operating out of the family's backyard, and by 1956 it had become obvious that a larger production space was needed. The Lladrós opened their first porcelain factory in 1958 on a lot attached to a house owned by the grandmother of José's wife, Carmen. The family successively expanded this first factory until the company outgrew it. Lladró completed work on its current factory complex in Tavernes Blanques in 1969, expanding it over time to a campus now so extensive that it is known as "Porcelain City."

What's important to note in this company growth is the astonishing speed with which it took place. Certainly, there were hard times—even, as José makes plain in his memoir, times of tension and disagreement among the brothers themselves. Nevertheless, by the end of the twentieth century, these three former farm boys had established themselves as the owners of an internationally famous business with expansive production facilities, significant real-estate holdings, export interests in countries around the world, and gross income in the many millions of dollars. One of the perks of such phenomenal success is that one gets noticed by—and is able to hobnob with—the rich, famous, and titled, and it is clear from company literature, including José Lladró's memoir, that such contacts were singularly important to three brothers who had grown up in poverty and obscurity.

Company founders rarely get to experience in their own lifetimes such a rapid rise to prominence. It is probably not accidental that the fantasy character of Cinderella makes so many appearances in the Lladró corpus (model #s 1493, 4828, 5957, 6364, 7553)—including her starring role in one of the most elaborate and expensive porcelain tableaux Lladró ever created, "Cinderella's Arrival" (#1785 G), at a last retail price of $33,000 USD. The opposite gender of its protagonist notwithstanding, the rags-to-riches Cinderella myth would have been one with which the Lladró brothers could very much identify.

Model of a Hispania parrot from the days predating Lladró's acquisition of that company. This figurine would have been very much the type of Hispania item the Lladró brothers would have included in their first retail shop in the early 1950s.

Rare Lladró-marked Thumper-style bunny from the early 1950s, more often (still rarely!) found paired in a model with Bambi-style fawn. Painting over surface glaze in a somewhat unrefined style, with eye painting beginning to show the wear vulnerability of overglaze painting. Courtesy of Brad Welch.

Variant of early Lladró, "Horse" (#277.12), sculpted by Fulgencio García. Originally owned by a close business associate of the Lladrós whom the Lladrós approached with a buyback request—and one of the models the then owner couldn't bring himself to part with. Courtesy of Janet Gale Hammer. $2,500–$3,000.

EARLY PRODUCTION AND MODEL HISTORY

The sculptor names most frequently associated with the Lladró figurine models produced in the 1950s are Fulgencio García, who was to remain with the company until his death in 1994, and Amparo Amador, whose name drops out of company production records in the early 1960s. Another sculptor identified as Antonio Arnal, whose name also disappears from future records, did all of his models in white porcelain. The earliest known Lladró model by García was a 1954 rabbit (model #55.04), on which the paint was applied over the glaze. By the end of that decade, Lladró would, pretty much exclusively, perfect and shift to a technique of underglaze painting as described later in this chapter.

The brothers believed in themselves enough to be confident their business venture would be successful, but it's probably fair to say they were blindsided by the enormity of that success and the need it would eventually generate for things such as model archives and collector catalogs. Consequently, the company did not keep early production records and, in most cases, didn't keep the models themselves but sold them to their early customers. As it gradually became clear that Lladró had a legacy to protect, the family found it necessary to approach some of these very early customers in an attempt to buy back rare examples of their own work. Not every customer they approached, however, was willing to part with these earliest Lladró treasures, some of which were made by the Lladró brothers themselves, and many of which were, for all intents and purposes, prototypic or one of a kind (or both).

The very earliest work by the Lladró brothers themselves was generally derivative of classical European styles, the imitation of early styles and forms being an approved tradition in the teaching and learning of young artists. It took some years for their company to develop that distinctive, elongated, Goyaesque look that would become a hallmark of Lladró design. Although company catalogs give 1969 as the starting year for model issues identified with a whole serial number, it is apparent that some of the best-known retail models from that era were introduced several years earlier. According to an article in an early edition of *Expressions*, a publication of the now-defunct Lladró Collectors Society, "Sad Harlequin" (model #4558 G/M) was already being successfully marketed by 1965.[5] As late as 1990, an edition of *Expressions* containing a short feature on sculptor Salvador Furió revealed, "His very first figurine, made for Lladró in 1964, was 'Clown with Concertina' (#1027)."[6]

The wording of this direct quote from a magazine produced by the company is interesting since it is apparent from earlier company literature that Fulgencio's "very first" cataloged model was at least a decade before 1964. It may be that Lladró was hiring its earliest collaborating sculptors on a freelance basis and that García and others who worked on the decimal-numbered earliest models were not actually employed by Lladró; it seems unlikely the brothers would have been in a position, in the mid-1950s, to hire the sculptors as permanent employees, even on a part-time basis.

Although José Lladró cites "Sad Harlequin" as having been the "breakthrough" model in what was to become a distinctive Lladró style,[7] it appears that the model's sculptor, Fulgencio García, may have had quite a lot in his own right to do with the evolution of that style, and even earlier than "Sad Harlequin." When we look at the photographs of García's work from the 1950s and early 1960s, we see the style already seminally present in his work. In models such as "Hawaiian" (#100.06) in 1959, "Saint Joseph" (#106.06) in 1959, "Nude with Dolphin" (#217.08) in 1958, and "Horse" (#277.12) in 1958, and especially in "Virgin [Mary]" (#302.13) in 1958, "Harlequin and Ballerina Lamp" (#245.10) in 1961, and "Country Girl" (#296.13) in 1961, García was already pushing the boundaries beyond the purely representational—was, in fact, already more than hinting at that elongation that would become a Lladró hallmark. The genius of the Lladró brothers was ever and always in recognizing entrepreneurial potential—in this instance, recognizing the possibilities in that elongated style and promoting and encouraging it as a characteristic attribute of Lladró figurines.

From the decade of the 1970s, retail catalogs were still available that allowed the company to say with a much-higher degree of certainty when a model was first issued. The oldest decimal-numbered items in the Lladró catalog, excluding those made in the 1940s by the brothers themselves, were made in the years 1953 through 1965, and each model was made in very small numbers. But for the first factory-made issues with whole serial numbers made in the years 1965 through 1969, the company seems to have chosen 1969 as a sort of default "year 1" for its production, perhaps for the significance of that year as the date when the current factory opened and also when the company began exporting to the United States, which, for decades to come, would be Lladró's biggest export market. It should be understood, then, that some models assigned to this "first issue" year for record reconstruction purposes were actually issued some years earlier.

Another García model, "Girl with Lamb" (#4505 G/M), issued ca. 1965–67. Not retired until 2001, its delicate modeling increases the risk that examples on the secondary market will be damaged/repaired around the lamb's ears or girl's neck. Sculptor: Fulgencio García. $125–$150.

Sevres-style urn, one of the few early works known to have been done by the Lladró brothers themselves. Made ca. 1944 and modeled by Vicente Lladró with flowerwork and painting by José and Juan. Courtesy of Brad Welch and Janet Gale Hammer at A Retired Collection, priced at $27,500.

Left to right near bottom:
Close-up of the cartouche painting of lady with rose on the face of the Sevres-style urn. Brad Welch says he had quite a time getting this urn, purchased at an auction in Spain, through US customs; specifically, it took time to convince them it wasn't an antique!

Close-up of the cherub finial with flowerwork on the detachable lid of the urn. Brad notes it must have taken the three brothers weeks to make this one urn with all its many details of modeling, painting, and decoration.

Old, hand-painted mark on the Sevres-style urn. This was the earliest form of Lladró mark, and while it might seem easily imitated, counterfeiters would be readily outed on quality grounds. (What counterfeiter would spend the time even if they could imitate the art?)

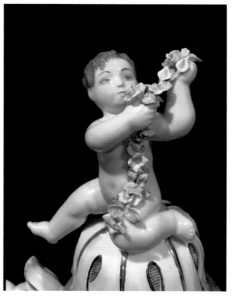

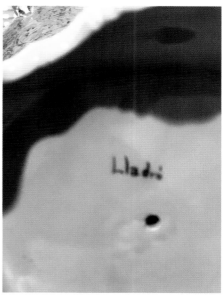

HOW A LLADRÓ IS MADE

Lladró porcelains are made in the time-honored tradition perfected by the Meissen company in the eighteenth century, using handmade techniques that have remained essentially unchanged since that time. Antique production techniques and handmade processes deflect the charge one sometimes hears that Lladró is "mass produced." It is worth remembering that even antique Meissen was produced in many copies of the same item, "so that [even] they are in some sense an instance of mass production."[8] However, what is involved in fine porcelain is quite a different measure of "mass" than several millions of industrial widgets or plastic whistles shooting out on a conveyor belt.

The Lladró production process begins with designs on paper that are then approved by (though not necessarily originating with) the Lladró family. These two-dimensional drawings are then rendered three-dimensionally in a clay sculpture, done in a size about a third larger than the intended figurine in order to allow for kiln shrinkage. After approval (or modification) of the sculpture by the Lladró family, it is cast in a hollow plaster form that can be cut up to use as production molds.

These individual molds for the various parts of the figurine are then filled with liquid porcelain "slip," which is allowed to harden. The number of molds needed for a given model varies with the size and complexity of the model. Fifteen to twenty molds are required on average to produce a Lladró. To give a more precise sense of the range, it took nine molds to make "All Aboard" (#7619 G, a 1992, Lladró Collectors Society "members only" model)[9] and 350 molds to make "18th Century Coach" (#1485 G)! The latter is a limited edition of 500 and, at a retail cost of $40,000 as of this writing, is one of the most complex and expensive groupings Lladró has ever made, consisting of a horse-drawn coach, four horses, a driver, two footmen, and a seated woman inside the coach, the entire tableau measuring more than 45 inches long.[10] Porcelain production is not like art glass production with iron molds that can be used again and again over many decades. Because Lladró molds are made of plaster, they can last for only about forty or fifty castings, after which new molds must be made in order to preserve the crispness of detail in the finished product.

Once removed from the molds and polished on the edges so that no seams will show at the joins, the porcelain parts are reassembled into the final figurine and adhered with porcelain slip. Unless the item is bisque (unpainted white), it next goes to be painted.

There are three possible ways to paint ceramics: "cold painting" over the glaze after firing (which tends to produce flaking over time, such as may be seen in many mid-twentieth-century American kitchen ceramics); painting over the glaze, which is then refired so that the paint fuses with the underlying material; and painting under the glaze, followed by firing. The painting method most often used by Lladró is the latter, painting under glaze, a technique first developed in China as early as the late thirteenth or early fourteenth century to produce its famous blue-on-white porcelain. In Spanish, the technique is called *bajo cubierto* (literally, "under cover").

Although Lladró might seem to use a narrow range of neutral pastels, its total palette actually includes more than 5,000 options for colors and color tones. The colors when first applied are surprisingly vivid, even garish. Lladró's characteristically bleached finished colors are a function of the way the raw paints interact chemically with the fire of the kiln. In order to reduce the amount of *unacceptable* variation in copies of a given model (*some* amount of variation between copies being part of the inherent charm of handmade products), painters specialize in

"Who's the Fairest?" (#5468 G/M), retired in 2000 at a last retail of $205. Value of the glazed version today: $250–$275, perhaps $50–$100 more for the matte version, retired in 1991. Also made in Gres (#2313). Sculptor: Juan Huerta.

"Josefa Feeding Her Duck" (#5201 G), sculpted by Francisco Catalá, is an unusually colorful Lladró model. Although we often associate it with a fairly narrow spectrum of neutral pastel grays and browns, Lladró actually uses thousands of colors and color tones. $200–$250.

Retired "Duck Seller" (#1267 G/M). The basket of ducklings was also spun off as a separate model, "Ducklings" (#4895 G/M), still in production. Sculptor: Juan Huerta. $175–$200.

Close-up of the "floret" pattern variant in enamel paint found on the kerchief of my example of "Duck Seller." Most examples of the model will have a plain white kerchief.

specific models, with the process prevented from becoming tedious for the artisans by the regular retirement of older models and the addition of new ones.

Consistent with Lladró's handmade production, collectors will note other minor variations from copy to copy of the same model—a little group of raised floral dots here and there on a girl's skirt or a line of dots accenting the collar or hemline on an angel's robe—as if the painters couldn't resist the occasional addition of an accent of their own. There are also color variations in cat and kitten models that evolve over time, some of a given model being painted in gray and white, others of the same model in tan and white. Leaf color may be a solid pale green in some versions of a model and striated with white in others. Generally speaking, these variations do not amount to "model variants" that would command any difference in secondary-market price.

There are exceptions to this rule, however, usually in the sports figurines and often involving not only a different uniform color in the variant but also the addition of the Lladró logo to the cap or sports shirt. These items are recognized as "official variants" and can command a price premium over the more common retail version of the same model.

Before firing, decorative accents such as parasols and separately articulated flowerwork are also applied with porcelain slip. Occasionally, one sees decorative elements applied with unsightly yellow glue, used on occasion even at the factory itself to salvage loose or detached accessories that may have come loose post firing, at which point molten slip could not have been used successfully. Since it is impossible to tell the difference between glue applied at the factory and an after-sale re-adhesion, and since dried glue tends to be unsightly in either case, collectors are advised to avoid, whenever possible, items with visible glue.

Lace is among the decorative accents used in older Lladró. This is actual lace that has been dipped in porcelain and then arranged around the figurine before firing (e.g., as hem ruffles or skirting or the "cloth" lining in a porcelain basket of flowers). When the item is fired, the underlying lace burns away, leaving only its porcelain outline. This method of producing porcelain lace dates from the early Meissen period and is often seen on antique Dresden figurines. Because this antique procedure results in extremely delicate decoration that is highly vulnerable to breakage, it was not often used, and, at least for antique German examples, collectors have been tolerant of minor damage. Lladró itself rarely used the technique after retiring its Caprichos series of porcelain flower arrangements in the late 1980s; these arrangements, which often contained lace, presented virtually insurmountable shipping challenges and frequently arrived broken at their retail destinations. Consequently, lace-lined Capricho flower baskets in perfect condition command a substantial premium on the secondary market.

Lladró parasols on its figurines are also made from lace panels sewn together to form the top and then dipped and arranged over a domed frame that helps the parasol retain its shape in the kiln. Ruffled edges of parasols are made from sewn lace dipped into the porcelain and then adhered to the rim. Once again, the underlying lace and stitching will burn away in the kiln, leaving only the porcelain shell.

Lladró flowerwork is likewise labor intensive, with each leaf, stem, petal, and stamen formed out of bits of colored porcelain and then adhered to a model individually to make flowers. Lladró is famous for the quality of its flowerwork, and there are Lladró artisans exclusively dedicated to the task. Because the work is so meticulous and time consuming, the addition of flowerwork on any model tends to increase its retail cost. There is also a price premium on pristine flowerwork for retired models purchased on the secondary market.

Once the main body of the figurine has been painted and all the major and minor elements have been adhered, a matte (unglazed) figurine is ready for the kiln. If the model is to be glazed, an additional step in the process uses a spray technique that assures an even glaze application and prevents excess glaze pooling that could obscure model detailing.

Figurines are batched for firing on large shelved carts that can be wheeled into the kiln. Batches are arranged according to the temperature and number of hours needed for firing. As an example, a smallish figurine such as "All Aboard" (model #7619) was fired for twelve hours at 1,320ºC.[11]

All of this tells us "why Lladró is so expensive." Lladró is made of fine porcelain, which has historically been considered a precious material. Lladró products are made by hand, using what are essentially antique processes (with some modern technological enhancements such as glaze spray machinery, kiln trucks, modern kilns, etc.). Each item requires multiple molds—and the molds themselves have to be replaced after relatively few castings. Decorative accessories are extremely labor intensive. The entire process of making even the simplest of individual Lladró figurines takes many hours.

DIFFERENCES IN CERAMIC MEDIA

"Fawn Surprise" (#6618 G), a Faberge-like egg, top lifting off to reveal a tiny reclining fawn amid Lladró flowerwork. One of a series of eggs containing animals, including "Puppy Surprise" (#6617 G) and "Kitty Surprise" (#6616 G), produced for three years, 1999–2001. Sculptor: Begoña Jauregui. $300–$325.

Lladró uses several kinds of surface finish for its figurines. Clear glaze applied before firing turns vitreous in the kiln, resulting in the high-gloss sheen commonly associated with Lladró. The effect of gloss is to give "glitz" to the model and to bring out the colors—no small contribution, given the neutral, faded pastels that Lladró favors. Matte surfaces are unglazed, the effect of which is to emphasize the modeling lines and details of the sculpture itself. While these modeling details appear sharper in the matte finish, the colors appear even more muted. Initially, Lladró often made the same model both in glazed and matte forms, though throughout the company's history, it has also made some models in only one or the other.

"Jolie" (#5210 G) carries a parasol, its top and edges made with lace sewn into panels and ruffles, then dipped in porcelain and arranged over a dome frame to keep their shape in the kiln, where the underlying lace burns away. Sculptor: José Puche. $300–$350.

The matte (unglazed) finish has generally been more popular in Europe than in the United States, perhaps because of the greater exposure of Europeans to ancient sculptures where matte surfaces were the norm. In the United States, Lladró's matte finish experienced fluctuating fortunes. In 1991, export sales of matte figures in the US were so lackluster that the manufacturer withdrew nearly all mattes then in production.

With this mass 1991 retirement, matte suddenly became scarce and desirable, with collectors who had come late to that party driving secondary-market prices on retired matte figurines even higher than those of their glazed counterparts. Retail production tended to rise and fall, with the company at times making more mattes and at other times fewer as it rode out the rollercoaster of market whim.

One of the unforeseen consequences of the mass 1991 matte retirement was that it frustrated the efforts of collectors of modest means to add to their matte Lladró Nativity and other multiple-model sets over time, thereby spreading the acquisition cost. When the matte versions of these sets were summarily retired, many collectors were left scrambling to complete their own sets, and this, too, drove prices up for at least some of the now relatively scarce matte items in Lladró's famous "Child Nativity" set (a.k.a. "Belen Nativity," model #s 4670–4680), which was produced in glazed versions as well.

There is a third Lladró finish called Gres. Actually, Gres was not just a different finish but an entirely different ceramic that was more akin to earthenware, and the formula for which is a closely guarded company secret. The slip itself is made in various earth-toned shades, making it especially suited to ethnic and nature themes. The painting process uses enamel over-paint that has been fired to fuse with the underlying ceramic. The unpainted matte surfaces of the ceramic contrast nicely with the smooth feel of the enamel paints.

As with mattes, Gres was more popular in Europe than in the United States. Because of the fondness of the company itself for this ceramic formula, Lladró periodically puts a marketing push on it at the retail level in the US, but it's been a hard sell, and relatively few Gres models circulate on the US secondary market.

One of the attractions of Gres is that it enables production of figurines in larger forms than is practical or possible with regular porcelain. (Porcelain doesn't lend itself to productions of monumental size—as the founders and artisans of the great Meissen company quickly discovered when the German imperial family wanted it to produce life-size animal models. It simply wasn't possible to get these through the kiln fire without damage, never mind what happened to them as they were subsequently exposed to changes in the atmosphere outside the kiln.) The large size of many Gres models makes them more suitable as table centerpieces than as shelf pieces. A limitation of Gres is that the rustic ceramic tends to resist the delicate detailing possible with regular porcelain, although Lladró did make some of its smaller Gres models in regular porcelain as well.

Lladró has also created several special series that have their own distinctive surface, among which I especially want to mention the Goyesca series, so named for its aesthetic affinities with the work of the painter Francisco Goya (1746–1828). The sculptor for the entire Goyesca series was Enrique San Isidro, famous in his own right as a contemporary Spanish painter and sculptor. In contrast to regular-porcelain-formula Lladró, where the porcelain is painted, the color in Goyescas is added to the ceramic itself, which is applied to the figurine in layers. The texture of clothing is achieved by pressing actual fabric into the porcelain before it hardens, which leaves behind the

"Pepita with Sombrero" (#2140), a 7-inch-tall Gres figurine retired in 2015 at a last retail price of $310, illustrates both the expense of producing Gres and its capacity to depict racial and ethnic identities beyond just Anglo-Europeans. Sculptor: José Puche.

Gres "Little Girl with Scarf" (a.k.a. "Missy," #4951), issued in 1976 and retired in 1985. Measures 16 inches tall by 6.5 inches at widest point and weighs in at 5 pounds. The tallest Gres tops out at just under 3 feet, much larger than possible in regular porcelain. Sculptor: Francisco Catalá. $700–$750.

"Rabbit's Food" (#4826 G/M), matte (unglazed) (*at left*) and glazed (*at right*). Sculptor: Vicente Martinez.

textile imprint. Because their production was so extraordinarily labor intensive, Goyescas were made in small-run limited editions that were expensive to purchase but quickly subscribed. They are no longer being made by the company and are scarce indeed on the secondary market, as discerning and well-heeled collectors hold onto the ones they have.

The Goyesca series is among the finest artistic achievements of the Lladró corpus. There are those who are inclined to find "regular collection" Lladró somewhat sentimental or "kitschy" (a pejorative that one sees once in a while, usually leveled by journalists who take their cues from other journalists, who have, in turn, based their impressions on exposure to a handful of Lladró's more commonly available small figurines). Such charges fall before any model ever produced in the Goyesca collection. In theme and treatment, the series is poignant and even dark. Sculptures such as "Little Boy" (#1696, whose title is more literally and appropriately rendered from the Spanish as "Addled Child") and "Mayoress" (#1799, the ultimate crone) are unforgettable in their impact—at once chilling and deeply moving.

"The Journey" (#3700), shown with limited-edition certificate, one of the happier-seeming items in sculptor Enrique San Isidro's incomparable Goyescas series. Edition size of 500 sold out within three years of its 1997 issue. Courtesy of Joëlle Ley. $850–$900.

WHAT MAKES A LLADRÓ A LLADRÓ?

Describing the making of a Lladró doesn't answer the question of what makes a Lladró inimitable in the deeper, more aesthetic, and less tangible sense. What are often cited as distinctive characteristics of the Lladró aesthetic are actually its least important aspects: high-gloss glaze and a muted pastel color palette. In these two aspects, Lladró is sufficiently like contemporaneous German and Scandinavian porcelains—the latter represented by the famous companies Royal Copenhagen and Bing & Grøndahl—as to be mistaken for them by amateur observers. Yet, there are evident differences between Lladró and these Nordic porcelains, even in these two aspects where they would seem to be most alike.

Lladró has perfected an even glaze application that obscures as little as possible of the model's underlying detail, whereas in the German and Scandinavian models, the glaze is sometimes so thickly applied as to pool and fill in much of the detail. In Royal Copenhagen porcelains, uneven glaze application can also result in unsightly glaze blisters on the eyes of larger animal figures.[12]

The literal English translation from the Spanish title of this Lhasa Apso (#4642 G/M) is "Moustaches." Retired in 1981. Sculptor: Salvador Furió. $300–$350.

The colors in Scandinavian and German porcelains are distinguishable from Lladró by their color tones; as appropriate to Nordic climates, the tones of blue and brown in Danish and German porcelains are cool and vivid. What are often described as the "neutral" pastels in Lladró are shades of blue, gray, and tan that look as if they'd been bleached by a warm Mediterranean sun.

What has caused the most confusion for amateur collectors, however, is not the similarity between Lladró and other European porcelains but, rather, product imitations from within Spain itself. By the 1980s, when it was clear to everyone that Lladró had become a hot commodity, small artisanal enterprises began to mushroom all over the Valencia region of Spain, most working "in the Lladró style" in preference to developing a style of their own. These upstart companies figured they could cut into Lladró's market by undercutting it on price, Lladró's one vulnerability. Competitors couldn't lower the price without debasing the artistic quality—and, in any case, their artisans manifestly lacked the skill to produce quality able to compete with Lladró's.

The true Lladró style has thus proven essentially inimitable. The technical risks that Lladró takes with the porcelain medium put it far out ahead of the pack that had hoped to nip at its heels. Lladró occupies space in unique ways, with parts such as arms, legs, and wings arcing out into thin air. These projecting parts are more vulnerable to breakage during production. They also require more production molds than a model tucked in upon itself, plus more technical skill in assembling the parts. For these reasons, competitor companies hoping to undercut Lladró on price, and using less skilled artisans to do so, simply will not take the technical risks that Lladró does. Competitors will not produce separately articulated fingers on a hand or allow an arm or leg to project out from the figure's main center of gravity.

Because of the way in which a Lladró model reaches into space, it has a dynamic quality that is exciting and occasionally uncanny. I am lucky enough to own the early "Hunting Dog" (#308.13, pictured in the introduction), made in 1963, a model so consummately flowing in its lines that every time I look at it, some corner of my mind half expects to see it trot right off the mantel. (Observant collectors will note that the bird in the dog's mouth is a quail and not the long-necked goose pictured in company catalogs. When I called Lladró's US headquarters several years ago to ask about this, I was told that the dog with quail was an even *rarer* variant than the one with the goose. But since few veteran collectors I know have ever seen the long-necked goose variant yet *have* encountered the version with the quail, it's fairly apparent the one with the goose is the rarer model.)

Extraordinarily dynamic Lladró groupings include the soccer players in "Shot on Goal" (#5879G) and the elegantly homing "Flock of Birds" (#1462). These are aesthetic and technical tours de force the like of which Lladró's competitors could never attempt.

On those many occasions when I am asked to authenticate an uncataloged Lladró, I always rely on faces as my ultimate determinant. Lladró faces are noted for the delicacy and the careful modeling of facial features such as eyes, noses, cheeks, and chins. Lladró uses subtle paint shades on faces, in a way that suggests

Below:
Front and back views of "Turtle Dove" (#4550 G/M), retired in 1998. At the back, where it will seldom be seen except in a 360-degree display space, one claw is separately articulated from the surrounding porcelain—a technical detail that sets Lladró apart. Sculptor: Fulgencio García. $275–$300.

facial features rather than calling attention to them. The use of coarse primary colors on eyes, eyebrows, and lips is a common failing of companies trying to imitate the Lladró style.

Another distinctive characteristic of Lladró is its diversity and inclusivity. Even though it occasionally flirts with stereotype, Lladró's reaching beyond the boundaries of Spain to appreciate the gifts of other cultures and to attempt to portray them in porcelain shouldn't be taken for granted. When we look at high-quality contemporaneous European porcelains, there is a certain nationalistic homogeneity that we associate with, say, Royal Doulton figurines or Bing & Grøndahl or Royal Copenhagen. Royal Doulton themes are specifically British, and part of the charm of Bing & Grøndahl or Royal Copenhagen is their single-minded focus on traditional Danish cultural themes and costumes. Given the provincial origins of the Lladró founders and their membership in the fairly homogeneous culture of the Spain in which they grew up—which is to say mainly white, Eurocentric, and (at least nominally) Roman Catholic—Lladró's global thematic outreach is extraordinary as well as singular among contemporaneous European porcelains.

As an early example, Lladró's production of six child angels (#s 4536–4541 G/M), which dates from the mid- to late 1960s, is unusual in several respects. Various attitudes shine forth on the faces of the angels, from innocence to mischief to petulance—the latter two attitudes not traditionally associated with angels but certainly apt for uncensored children. The series also includes one black angel and one Asian angel. That might not seem like much of a nod to diversity in a time when we have come pretty much to expect it, but back in the mid- to late 1960s, it would have been considered, in many parts of the world (including the United States), revolutionary, not to say heretical, to attribute to angels any race other than white.

Many Lladró figures or figure sets also have a narrative quality to them. One of my favorite examples is "Honey Lickers" (a.k.a. "Sweety," model #1248, see p. 33). This little tableau features a small girl with a mischievous expression on her face. She is seated on a hassock and holding a honey pot, into which she is dipping her finger. The pot is painted on the side with the Spanish word for honey, *miel*. Three frisky Dalmatian pups surround her, each with its own sweet tooth and waiting for a taste.

In the first place, I love the aesthetic angles of the piece, which incorporate a number of spatial triangles (formed, for example, by the girl and the puppies, the position of her legs relative to her lap, the position of her arms and torso, and the two little pigtails jutting out from her head). But I'm also tickled by the figurine's narrative punch line, to be found in that puppy at the base, who seems to find his sweetness not in the honey but in the girl's big toe. It's too cute only in the sense that reality is too cute; one can imagine such a tableau in a sweet moment of real life, which is part of what gives this grouping its special charm.

We can cite again Lladró's Child Nativity set, not only for its racial inclusivity but for its gender inclusivity and even its subversive narrative aspects. The idea of letting children stand in for the Nativity figures is not unique to Lladró, but Lladró's treatment of that approach is. In the first place, two of the shepherds are girls, and at least one of the kings (the kneeling one) is sufficiently androgynous as to be gender indeterminate. The Baby Jesus lies naked, asleep on a pillow, turned on his side with his cheek in his hand and a sleepy smile on his face—hardly the typically pious and swaddled pose attributed to him in the more traditional Nativity tableaux. (See, for example, the Christ Child pictured here in Salvador's Furió's lovely but more conventional interpretation of the Nativity, where the baby's hand is raised as if he were already preparing to impart his first divine

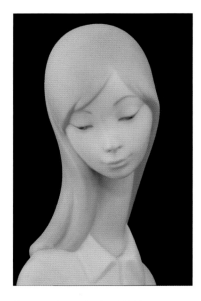

Close-up of facial detail on "Girl Student" (Lladró model #4518 G/M and also found with impressed NAO mark). Note the delicacy of detail and lack of dark colors or coarse brushstroke in lips and eyes. The quality of facial painting is one of the authenticity "tells" for Lladró brands.

"My New Pet" (#5549) is part of a series of models of African American children Lladró produced in the 1980s and early 1990s. This one was issued in 1989 and retired in 1998. Sculptor: Juan Huerta. Estimated value: $200–$225.

Top left:
"Black Angel" (#4537 M) and "Angel Praying" (#4538 G), issued in the 1960s, from a series of six child angels, five of which remain in glazed production 50 years later. In attributing to an angel race other than Caucasian, Lladró was ahead of its time. Series sculptor: Fulgencio García.

Top right:
"Angel with Horn" (#4540) and "Chinese Angel" (#4536). The Chinese Angel is the only one of the series of six child angels in the series to have been completely retired (in 2004)—perhaps because it inspired the most questions among collectors (e.g., "Why is the Chinese Angel bald?").

Bottom:
Left to right, "Angel Thinking" (#4539) in glaze and "Angel Reclining" (#4531) in matte. "Cheekiest" and most amusing is that reclining angel with the bored expression. Current retail on glazed versions is $150—and at that price, may be cheaper on the secondary market.

"Mary" (#4671 G/M) and "Saint Joseph" (#4672 G/M) in traditional postures. *Somebody* has to uphold piety—but certainly not this "Baby Jesus" (#4670), asleep on a pillow, wearing nothing but a smile. (Lladró's "Miniature Kitten" [#5307 G] is an addition to my Nativity display: what is a stable without a cat?)

"Sweety" (a.k.a. "Honey Lickers" or "Sweet Tooth," #1248 G/M). Sculptor: Juan Huerta. $400–$450. The puppies were also spun off as individual items and are surprisingly expensive as stand-alones in the secondary market: as much as $200 or more apiece.

blessing.) In the Child Nativity set, children bring the Christ child not the traditional royal gifts of gold, frankincense, and myrrh but the gifts a baby could love and delight in: a wrapped present, a toy truck, a teddy bear.

The most regal of the three kings, the one who looks as if he might actually be a king, is the little black boy. And although one of the shepherd girls may merely be standing in the saucy, exaggerated posture often adopted for Lladró figurines of female children, more than one observer has noted that she looks distinctly pregnant. The narrative here seems to tell us that the "child nativity" may really be a Nativity for adults, challenging traditional adult assumptions and subverting traditional theological expectations—reminding, us, perhaps, that Jesus came for "the little people," the poor and the outcast, whose company he always seemed to prefer to that of the pious. (Owing perhaps to these eccentricities of the set, one of its characteristics is that its individual models can stand alone thematically and, consequently, are often found as single items on the secondary market.)

Left to right:
"Shepherdess with Rooster" (#4677 M), "Shepherd with Lamb" (#4676G), "Shepherdess with Basket" (#4678 G) from the 11-piece "Child Nativity." ("Miniature Cocker Spaniel" [#5310 G] not sold as part of set but added to my Nativity display—because what little boy doesn't love a dog?)

The kings carry toy gifts fit for a Christ who was a real child. *Left to right,* "King Gaspar" with toy truck (#4674 G/M), "King Melchior" with a wrapped mystery gift (#4673 G/M), and "King Balthasar" with teddy bear (#4675 G/M).

Animals of the "Child Nativity," "Donkey" (#4679 G/M) and "Cow" (#4680 G/M), are, as fitting for the child-centered set, infant animals rather than full-grown versions usually seen in a Nativity tableau. Sculptor for this Nativity set: Juan Huerta. All Nativity models sold separately at retail. Value range for any piece: $100–$200.

Another model with a story to tell is "Girl with Pigeons" (#4915), which, at first glance, appears to be just a model of a peasant girl with a pair of white doves, one of them held tenderly to her breast. But as with so many Lladró figurines, it takes a second look to see that the details in the grouping don't quite fit the ostensible theme. The clue is the girl's foot stretched provocatively from under her dress. Notice the fancy footwear, then notice the frilly hem of the petticoat and ask what *those* are doing on a farm girl. I am disinclined to attribute this apparent mismatch to artistic carelessness or self-indulgence, since my experience of Lladró models is that detailing is nearly always the object of careful reflection and deliberation. As it happens, there was a tradition of masquerade balls among eighteenth-century German courtesans in which "dressing down" was a popular theme, parties in which the high-born dressed as peasants. The royal hosts of these affairs often purchased, as table decorations for the party feast, Meissen figurines depicting these "role reversals."[13] It's entirely likely that Lladró sculptors would have been familiar with this aesthetic tradition in reference to this model, especially given that tradition's connection to Meissen as the marker by which all European fine porcelain is judged.

"Girl with Pigeons" (#4915 G/M), a model of a peasant girl feeding pigeons, seems thematically unremarkable save for the extraordinary tenderness with which she holds one bird to her breast. But wait . . . Is this a rich girl dressing down or peasant girl dressing up? Sculptor: Salvador Debón. $175–$200.

Some academics have pointed to what Ricard Ramon Camps of the University of Valencia has termed an "aesthetics of innocence" in Lladró, as evidenced, for example, in its focus on childhood themes and the licensing collaboration between Lladró and Disney for some of the latter's most iconic characters (e.g., Cinderella and Snow White). It is an aesthetic, according to these experts, steeped in a pretend world in which good and evil are clearly distinguishable from one another, and in which good always wins out.[14]

Again, such judgments seem to me based on a lack of familiarity with the Lladró corpus as a whole. For a darker narrative, we can look to "Deer Hunt" (#4521 G) or "Hunting Scene" (#1238 G), both of which feature dogs attacking a terrified stag, or the Gres limited edition "Rescue" (#3505) with its boatload of slickered and anxious men rowing on a dangerous sea. These groupings and others, such as the Goyesca models previously mentioned, expose the shallowness of any journalistic analysis of Lladró as "saccharine." Sentimental these tableaux are most certainly not! Like any good art, Lladró reminds us of the beauty and innocence in the world, but it also reminds us that sometimes, truth is neither beautiful nor innocent.

A GALLERY
of Early, Rare,
and Uncataloged
LLADRÓ

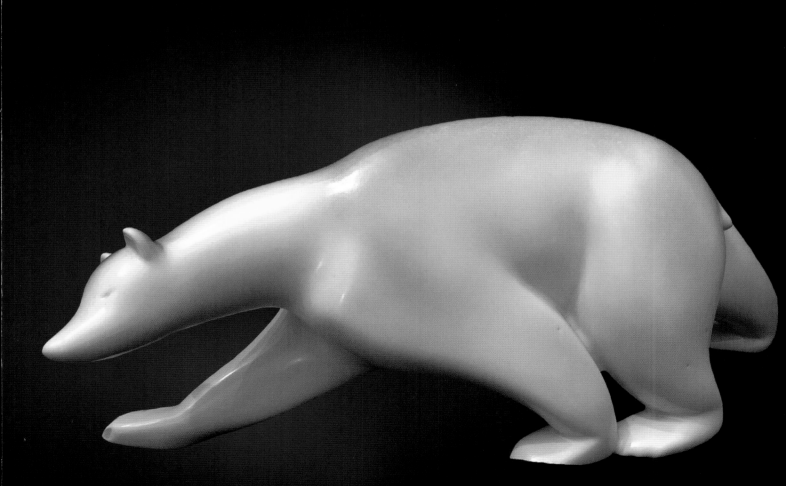

Collector Brad Welch is internationally known in the Lladró field and was kind enough to share with readers some photos from his unsurpassed collection, which contains many very early and, in some cases, one-of-a-kind Lladró models, some of which are pictured elsewhere in this book. Unless otherwise indicated, photos in this gallery section are from Brad Welch's collection (a gallery of known Lladró models follows chapter 2 of this book).

Two same-model ballerinas, one decorated, one nude. Painting style dates these to the 1950s, probably early in that decade. Dresden-style ballerinas with delicate lace skirts fully intact as here are rare as hen's teeth, and this model in that condition may well be one of a kind. Value undetermined.

This uncataloged, unnumbered bear on rocks is unusual among Lladró models in that the bear is brown instead of white.

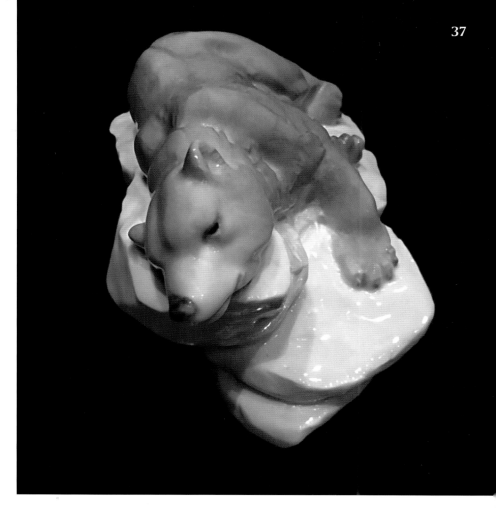

Below:
In 1983, Lladró collaborated with French glassmaker Daum Nancy to produce polar bear models in clear and frosted crystal. "Polar Bear Observing" (see image at bottom) was, apparently, the model for frosted "Crystal Bear" #C4502. Courtesy of Teresa K. Schmitt. Back order priced at $500 at A Retired Collection.

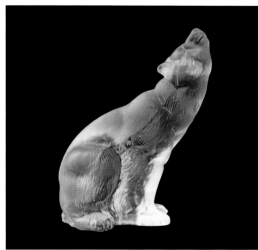

"Polar Bear Observing" (NAO model #75 G), a very early retirement in 1971, sometimes seen with Lladró mark but rarely found in either. Anatomical detail shows the capacity of Lladró sculptors for going beyond the merely "cute" in animal portrayals. Sculptor: Fulgencio García. Value undetermined.

An uncataloged Lladró deer grouping. That tall tree trunk makes me think this was probably conceived as a potential lamp model that was never released.

This smile-inducing, uncataloged Lladró model of a whimsical Siamese cat must be related to Lewis Carroll's Cheshire Cat! Sculptor unknown. Value undetermined.

Uncataloged woman with fish basket accompanied by boy with sailboat marked Lladró but never released in the core collection. It was, though, later released as Zaphir #672, retired in 1980, then again as NAO with the same model number, now also retired. Lladró-marked version at A Retired Collection priced at $1,800.

Here's another uncataloged, Lladró-marked item that would later emerge as a Zaphir, in this instance as "The Woodcutter" (Zaphir #552 G/M), though this one did not make a third incarnation as a NAO. Sculptor unknown. Value undetermined.

"Girl's Head" (#5090), one of several Lladró head busts, this one issued in 1980 and retired the following year. Sculptor: Vicente Martinez. It's back-ordered at $400 on A Retired Collection (which means not only that Janet Hammer doesn't have it now but that she probably has customers looking for it).

When Brad Welch bought this gorgeous lion's head at the factory, he assumed it was the prototype for what would become a sculpture release in the main line, but it never showed up again. Sculptor unknown. Value undetermined.

Lladró sometimes took commissions from other companies, in this case Vespa, late 1970s. Scooter later reprised in "Country Girl with Vespa" (#5143 G), 1982–1987, rider reaching back to a basket of flowerwork. Because of special, limited distribution, the scooter by itself would today be practically impossible to find. Value undetermined. Courtesy of A Retired Collection.

This is a book about figurines, but I'm including this very early canister set just because it's fun! Instead of the usual canister names in the US, the labels on these reflect the culture where they were produced (translated, *left to right*): sugar, rice, and chickpeas (a.k.a. garbanzo beans). Value undetermined.

Base on a canister shows a fairly sophisticated backstamp without logo. It indicates region but lacks country of origin, required on items produced for export. From that mark information, we can conclude that the set was among the brothers' earliest retail offerings before they were fully operational as an exporting company.

CHAPTER 2

THE LLADRÓ CORE COLLECTION:
Considerations and Caveats

Each thematic category in the Lladró "core collection" (as the main Lladró-marked collection is commonly called) has its own strong collector following; most collectors have found it necessary to specialize according to their own interests in order to avoid going broke!

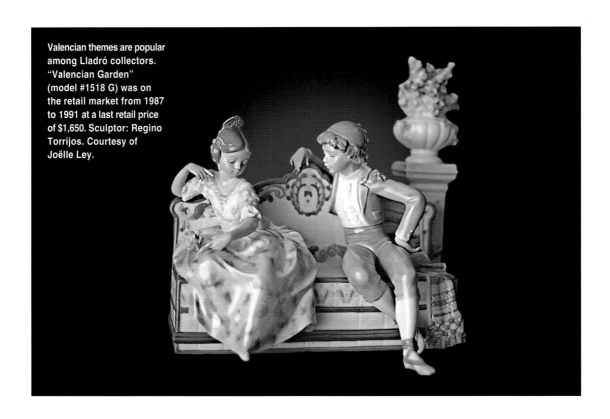

Valencian themes are popular among Lladró collectors. "Valencian Garden" (model #1518 G) was on the retail market from 1987 to 1991 at a last retail price of $1,650. Sculptor: Regino Torrijos. Courtesy of Joëlle Ley.

Among the most popular collecting categories in Lladró are animals, birds, Valencians in costume, elegant ladies, ballet dancers, and clowns. A person could also amass a substantial collection based on any of the following themes: angels, children with animals, babies, holidays (Christmas and Nativity and Easter), Jewish history and traditions, mermaids, other fantasy figures (elves, fairies, unicorns, et al.), harlequins, musicians, Asian cultures, and African and African American cultures.

"Circus Sam" (#5472 G) was issued in 1988 and is still in production at a retail price of $300 (up from its initial retail of $175!). Sculptor: Francisco Catalá.

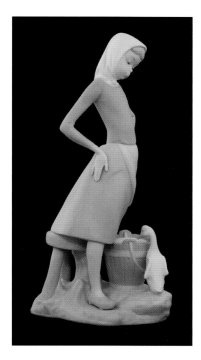

"Girl with Milk Pail" (#4682 G/M), here in matte, in Lladró's famously elongated style—and a narrative punch line as a duck boldly cops a drink while an exasperated but indulgent farm girl looks on. Both matte and glazed versions were retired in 1991. Sculptor: Vicente Martinez. $150–$225.

Collecting by theme is only one option, however. It's also possible to collect by porcelain type. Some collectors focus their acquisitions on matte figurines, others on Gres. Because both of these are relatively scarce on the secondary market, they tend to be self-limiting enough that a collector can specialize in either and not break the bank. A third option is collecting by production period or style—say, only figurines retired before 1970 (or 1980 or 1990) or only figurines made in the elongated style of older Lladró.

After you've been collecting for a while, you'll probably also find that you're drawn to the work of a particular sculptor or sculptors. I have a special fondness for the works of Fulgencio García and Juan Huerta, and I also very much like the miniature and precision detailing in the work of Antonio Ramos. One of my fellow collectors and photo contributors to this book is especially drawn to the work of Salvador Furió. Whatever your favorite Lladró sculptors, you'll find plenty of their work to keep you collecting for years to come (see appendix 2 for an annotated list of known sculptors, including representative examples of their work).

Although most of the staff working in the decorating and design department are women, Lladró has less than a handful of female sculptors (e.g., Joan Coderch, Begoña Jauregui, Virginia Gonzalez, and the NAO sculptor Eva Maria Cuerva). Surface appearances can be deceptive, however. Lladró sculptors, whatever their gender, are noted for their sympathetic and appreciative portrayals of women and girls, and they seem to have a particular skill for capturing the saucy playfulness of healthy girls. (I've often thought this may have had something to do with the fact that several of the second-generation Lladró offspring were little girls, who, with their brothers, notoriously had the run of the plant and would have provided ready material "on the fly" for artistic studies of girls behaving naturally.) By contrast, many of Lladró's figures of boys and men seem less animated, even stilted. This has caused some to claim that, as one female staffer at an authorized retail dealer once put it to me, "Lladró is prejudiced, you know, in favor of girls."

AUTHENTIC MARKS OF THE CORE COLLECTION

The oldest Lladró brand marks were either painted, hand etched, or machine impressed into the porcelain base. (See appendix 1 for photos of authentic Lladró brand marks.) For the core collection, hand-etched marks may include the full name Lladró or the initials LL over a P (standing for Porcelanas Lladró). The country of attribution may be Spain, Espain, or España. Once the decision was made to export to the United States, the Spanish-language country name España would not have been used in Lladró marks because the McKinley Tariff Act requires that the name of the country of origin be in English. Therefore, any item with España in the mark predates 1969, the year Lladró began exporting its products to the US. (When attempting to say English words that begin with an s, Spanish-speaking people will often add an e in front of the word, because in Spanish, there are few, if any, nouns that begin with the letter S; the most frequently occurring vowel before an s in a Spanish noun is the vowel e—hence, the misspelling of the English word Spain in early Lladró marks as "Espain.")

The blue backstamp came into use ca. 1972 and is actually applied with a paint chip that unfurls in the kiln to reveal the mark. The Lladró blue backstamp has gone through several decades of evolution, from simplicity to clutter and back to simplicity then cluttered again; despite efforts to streamline the look of the blue mark in the 1990s, the addition of successive elements (such as the quality assurance number added around year 2000) means that the mark remains fairly busy. In comparison, early blue backstamps, containing only the bellflower logo, the name Lladró, and "Made in Spain," seem almost naked in comparison, causing some to conclude "they must be seconds." On the contrary, these are simply the oldest genuine Lladró that are marked with a blue backstamp.

The copyright date in marks used from 1977 onward can be confusing. For earlier issues still retailing, this date is of little use in determining how long the item has been in production, because 1977 is simply the first year that designs were copyrighted. So if something was first issued in the mid- to late 1960s and came out of the kiln before 1977, it will have no date in the mark, while post-1977 firings of the same model will have a 1977 copyright date. However, copyright dates can be used to locate the issue year for later (post-1977) models. For items first issued after 1977, the copyright date is generally the year *before* first issue. For example, a model with a 1981 copyright date was first issued in 1982, a year 2000 copyright means the model was first issued in 2001, and so on. (First-issue and copyright years should not be confused with a given example's firing in the kiln; a popular model may be in production for many years, but its copyright date will still be based on the first issue of that model.)

Unless an item is a time-limited edition available for only one year, it's impossible to say with any precision just when a given example of a model was fired in the kiln. However, the marks and backstamps can be used to identify eras of production for particular models, at least within a range of years, and, thus, to tell early/older firings from late/newer ones. This can itself be used as a collecting principle; when an item is produced over a long period, I try to find, on the secondary market, items with impressed marks or the first backstamp.

One final issue needs to be mentioned with respect to marks. I mentioned that backstamps are applied with a paint chip that "unfurls" in the kiln. Sometimes, these don't unfurl completely, resulting in what I call a "dangling mark." Usually, there is enough of the mark visible that one can tell the item is genuine, and such not-completely-unfurled stamps don't have a negative impact on value.

There are many myths circulating about what does and does not constitute an authentic mark of a first-quality Lladró. When I first began collecting, I quickly learned all I could about the Lladró mark. People who'd been collecting a lot longer than I told me all sorts of tales that all basically amounted to the same claim: anything that didn't have a cobalt blue backstamp wasn't "a real Lladró." Such collectors routinely passed over old and valuable figurines because they didn't realize the oldest marks were etched or impressed, not color stamped (see appendix 1 at the end of this book).

Recently, I heard a variation on this theme, apparently a rumor widely circulating in Europe, that any cobalt-blue mark without the serial number impressed into the base is a "second." In fact, Lladró didn't begin impressing model numbers into the base until the early 1980s; consequently, anything fired in the 1970s or earlier wouldn't have the model number on the base at all.

Clearly, interpreting the mark is sometimes a case of "a little knowledge is a dangerous thing."

IDENTIFYING SECONDS

The term "seconds" refers to items that, for whatever reason, the manufacturer has deemed not quite up to its standards for release onto the retail market. The reason for the manufacturer's decision will generally not be evident to the eyes

"Duck" (#1056 G), a simple early model issued ca. 1966–67. Retired in 1978 (at a last retail of just $65), just before Lladró's popularity crested in the United States. It has the original blue backstamp: just bellflower, name, Made in Spain. Sculptor: Julio Fernandez.

Uncataloged Lladró seated dog with an old, impressed Lladró mark. It's the sort of genuine article that would be passed over as a fake by those who know a little bit but not enough about the Lladró mark and its evolution. Sculptor unknown. $750–$1,000.

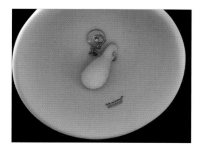

As an example, this 1989 Christmas bell is, on today's secondary market, the most expensive of the first series of Lladró Christmas bells produced from 1987 to 1996, valued at about $85 to $100—but not with this mark! The logo scrape decreases the value to $25 or less.

of those outside the company. In the case of Lladró, there may be what someone at the factory concluded was an unacceptable color variation. Also, because the models are handmade, even tiny variations in the proportions of facial features can result in a facial expression too far off the mark of the model's original intent to pass quality inspection (it's sometimes a fine line in facial expression between mischievous and demonic!).

Anything that comes out of the kiln with gross defects is, of course, destroyed before it ever gets onto the market. But seconds—those items not deemed "ready for prime time"—are sold in many industries, including, for example, famous-name clothing and leather goods; one often sees these items offered for sale in manufacturers' discount outlets. In the history of porcelain, seconds have a long and venerable tradition and have been sold by virtually every famous porcelain brand, including Meissen. Seconds sold at a discount are a means for manufacturers to recoup some of the expensive production costs for items with quality defects so minor they may not even be evident to a consumer. Consumers who buy seconds are generally casual visitors to company factories, perhaps on a tourist junket, or individuals who love the brand but can't afford the full retail price of a first-quality item. Particularly for casual buyers, this means they (or their families, in the case of an estate) don't have much attachment to the item, and that's how seconds end up on the secondary market.

Second-quality merchandise is offered at a discount at the initial retail point of sale; that reduced retail price means that a second will never have, over its lifetime, the value of a first-quality example of the same item, so it's important to be able to identify a second when you see one. Each porcelain company has its own way of marking seconds. Meissen seconds are indicated by two parallel hash marks scratched through the "crossed swords" of its famous logo. Royal Copenhagen (RC) indicates seconds with a single vertical hash mark scratched through the blue waves under the primary company mark. In comparison to RC seconds, where the hash mark is often subtle enough to be missed unless one tips the item at various angles so that the light hits it just right, Lladró seconds are clearly marked as such by scraping off of the entire "bellflower" logo above the name, usually with the erasure mark also clearly visible.

However, Lladró has historically had two or three "outlet" stores in the US, and, unfortunately, it uses these outlets to sell perfectly good, first-quality *overstock* from which company employees *also* scrape off the logo. These are also sold at deep discounts off retail. Because it is notoriously difficult for anyone outside the company to determine *why* a second was classified as such, it's usually impossible to tell the difference between a Lladró second and a first-quality item sold at an outlet on which the mark has been defaced in the same manner.

Serious collectors will, therefore, not buy anything with a defaced mark—with one exception. The factory in Spain has also sold prototypic models—unique items that never went into production—that it may have run as an internal company "test" for a decision about whether to take the model to market. These items are also marked with the logo scrape, but serious collectors love to have them because of their one-of-a-kind status. It is not advised that any amateur collector, however, bet the farm on distinguishing between a second and a prototype. Unless the collector is vastly familiar with the inventory of known Lladró models and knows the exact retail provenance of the item, chances are overwhelming that what the collector has found on the secondary market or in a family estate is a "second" or a "gray market" example of a cataloged model, not a prototype.

An exception to the logo scrape rule: Lladró made several highly decorated eggs, many of which their current owners purchased directly at the Lladró factory. Such items never went into production, and their logo was scraped off at the factory to prevent retail confusion. Courtesy of Brad Welch.

GRAY-MARKET MERCHANDISE

Historically, Lladró has used its own system of tightly controlled, authorized retail dealerships for the sale of first-quality items, a system that enabled the manufacturer to dictate everything from the retail price of the product to how it was displayed in the store. I actually have a copy of an official dealer's loose-leaf-bound Lladró manual stipulating the rules for how items were to be displayed, acceptable and unacceptable uses of the Lladró logo and logotype in sales materials, and so on. In the face of the multiple requirements, it was not unusual for prospective retail dealers to say, "No, thanks!" to carrying Lladró in their shops.

These days, most Lladró retail sales have been consolidated into "Lladró Centers" located in the urban glitz and glamour capitals of the world where the Lladró company actually owns the real estate. One of Lladró's reasons for consolidating its retail inventory into spaces it actually owns is the evolution of what's come to be called the "gray market" in Lladró. As the name implies, this isn't quite the black market, but neither is it strictly on the up and up. In this gray market, unauthorized dealers were able to open a supply pipeline of current-issue Lladró figurines and set their own prices, usually well below the company's "suggested retail" (which, in the authorized network, was never merely suggested but was mandated). This had the effect not only of cutting into Lladró's authorized retail sales but also of undercutting what has always been an important aspect of the product's appeal: its exclusivity.

Lladró suspected that the pipeline for this gray market was the authorized dealer network itself, whether marginal dealers wanting to get out of the Lladró business altogether or more-stable dealers perhaps merely wanting to offload excess merchandise they hadn't been able to sell. The "Lladró Center" consolidation strategy was, among other things, a means of plugging that pipeline after the company's litigation against gray-market dealers proved unsuccessful.

The Lladró company had previously had a fair degree of success in US courts, litigating such issues as copyright infringement, unauthorized use of the company name, and the like. Lladró's first real loss in the courts was when it sued to prevent retail sellers from acquiring Lladró merchandise from outside the company-authorized network. To distill the US Court of Appeals ruling on the issue, the plaintiff's case was not upheld because, the court said, retail dealers in the United States could not all be expected, with an imported product such as Lladró, to be able to tell the difference between merchandise acquired from Lladró-authorized import sources and import sources not authorized by Lladró.[1]

In the aftermath of the company's failed legal attempts to stop it, the gray market has been left to itself to flourish. Such dealers have mostly agreed to cooperate with the manufacturer to the extent of scraping off the logo or other sections of the mark to indicate that the item did not come from an authorized source. Unfortunately, as in the case of the Lladró company's own discount outlets, these logo scrapes involve defacing the mark on first-quality merchandise. It is important to know this because many of the Lladró items that are flooding eBay™ (with a consequent general depression in the secondary-market value of Lladró products) are being offered by gray-market sellers who continue to insist that they are selling "first quality" merchandise. The point is that no matter how pristine the item was *before* the mark was defaced, the defacement *now* renders the item damaged for collecting purposes. In other words, because serious collectors consider the mark to be integral to the item, tampering with it defaces not only the mark but the entire object.

"Natural Wonder," found at a "gray market" discount department store and purchased for considerably less than its authorized dealer price. Fortunately, it didn't have the logo scraped off. This model had a short production run from 1996 to 1999 at a last retail price of $220. Sculptor: Miguel Angel Santaeulalia.

To summarize, then, there are four categories of Lladró where the logo or other portion of the mark may be removed after manufacture with a visible scraping:

1 At the company's discount outlets (logo removed by company or outlet personnel)

3 At gray-market retail venues (logo removed by the gray market retailer)

2 At the Lladró factory in Spain (logo removed by the manufacturer)
   a. Discounted cataloged items the company is trying to move from excess inventory
   b. Prototypic items that never went into production

4 To indicate seconds (logo removed at the factory)

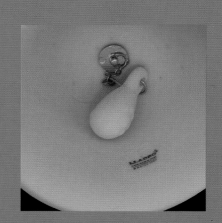

Of these, only items in category 2b are considered valuable by serious collectors, and those who aspire to a first-quality collection will avoid the rest.

HOW TO SPOT A COUNTERFEIT

Because of the potentially lucrative payoff for scammers, altered-mark merchandise isn't the only challenge for collectors. Counterfeiters are attracted to "luxury products" such as Lladró like ants to a picnic. Imitators, by contrast, are companies using their own marks (perhaps merely hoping the consumer won't notice). Imitations are riffing off the Lladró style, but counterfeiters are ripping off the Lladró name. Counterfeits are distinguished from imitations by the intent; using a bogus Lladró mark, counterfeiters fully intend to deceive consumers into thinking an item is the real article.

Because early production history for the company had to be reconstructed some twenty years after the fact, many genuine models simply fell through the holes in that net. Still, finding an item that is not included in the known catalog should be a red flag for a possible counterfeit. This is especially the case for models such as clowns, ballerinas, and other popular themes, since counterfeiters will generally try to leverage their risk by producing items in popular themes that would have the highest payoff and leverage against the risk of getting caught and prosecuted for forgery. Counterfeiters will confine themselves to simple, single-element models that rip off the most-popular Lladró themes in relatively simple forms with which they'd be most likely to fool an unsuspecting consumer. Generally speaking, counterfeiters will not attempt exact copies of known models in these themes, simply because the crooks aren't skilled enough to do so convincingly.

The process of identifying counterfeits is complicated by the evolution of the genuine mark, from old impressed marks scratched in by hand to machine-impressed marks to various iterations of the cobalt-blue Lladró backstamp and logo. Still, there will usually be something substantially "off" about a counterfeit mark. Because collectors who are only partly knowledgeable tend to be suspicious

Three Lladró girls arranged around a triangular bowl never went into production. The owner bought it at the factory, thinking it was a preproduction piece for a future issue, but it turned out to be a one of a kind. Logo flower removed. Value undetermined. Courtesy of Brad Welch.

of hand-etched or embossed marks anyway, counterfeiters generally try to copy a cobalt backstamp instead (e.g., where they think they can reduce the grounds for argument and fool a consumer who isn't looking too closely).

The Lladró stamp, while tightly compact, has distinct elements that are usually legible even through paint chip bleeding. Generally speaking, counterfeiters are neither very patient nor especially smart and will often not take the time to adequately study that which they're trying to forge. Consequently, they'll often "fudge" what they consider to be minor elements in the mark—for example, using a nondescript hash or accent mark where a copyright symbol should be. Even the accent mark on the *o* in the company name can be a tip-off. The genuine accent is usually quite distinctive, with a little left-leaning tail at the end of it, and the accent will usually not be touching the *o*. A counterfeit will often have a blocky-looking accent hash that will be directly touching the *o*. The logo may also be drawn inaccurately.

Finally, the color of the backstamp in a regular collection/core-brand Lladró should be cobalt blue, not mulberry, dark purple, sky blue, or black. Surprisingly, it's that precise shade of cobalt blue in a genuine Lladró backstamp that is apparently among the hardest things to forge (although I can't say why, since a color pretty much identical to it has been used by other Valencian porcelain makers that make their money by imitating the Lladró style if not its quality).

Unfortunately, efforts to educate collectors also potentially educate counterfeiters, so we can probably expect them to become more sophisticated in their efforts to duplicate the mark. Two other tips for spotting a counterfeit are sloppy model painting and integration of the main coloring of the model into the porcelain itself. Generally speaking, Lladró uses, in its regular non-Gres collection, a white porcelain slip, which it then paints. But that requires artisanal skill, which is generally in very short supply among figurine forgers. Human flesh tones, whatever the racial depiction of the model, are among the hardest colors to imitate successfully. It's much easier and cheaper for a counterfeiter to make the porcelain itself Anglo flesh colored and then produce items only with that racial profile than to try to paint the porcelain accurately (of course, since this last tip would be evident only upon damage to the figurine, it is not recommended as a test where there is any possibility the item might be genuine!).

CONDITION AND RESTORATION

Two questions I get frequently from other collectors are "How much does damage affect value?" and "Is it worth repairing?" In most cases, the answer to the first question is "quite a lot," unless the item in question happens to be a rarity not otherwise available. I mentioned in chapter 1 that Lladró is in some sense "mass produced," meaning that, for most retail items, a few thousand copies of the same model are potentially available worldwide. Consequently, knowledgeable collectors will not buy a damaged example as long as they believe they can get a pristine one instead.

A discerning collector will also distinguish between a manufacturing flaw and a damage defect. Collectors are generally tolerant of the former (unless it is grossly distracting); of the latter, not so much. Manufacturing flaws can be anything from glaze defects (a tiny missed spot or pinpricks in the glaze) to firing cracks. The firing crack will usually be separated into two edges so that there's a very narrow, jagged space running between the edges. Usually, firing cracks would not compromise the structural integrity of the model. I have,

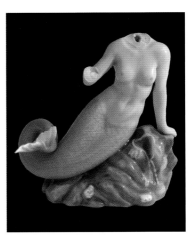

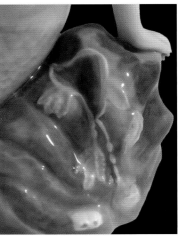

Counterfeit Lladró mermaid in "as found" condition, absent head and arm. Note the flesh color of the porcelain; with few exceptions, Lladró's regular porcelain would be white, then painted. Notice the poor painting quality in the rock where the mermaid sits and the two crude dots on the breasts.

Counterfeit mark on the base of the forged mermaid. Note the mulberry color (which looks very nearly black on the actual object), the general fuzziness of the lettering, and the "tail" off the top of the *o* where a separate copyright sign should be.

"Eskimo Playing with Bear" (#1195 G/M), retired in 2000, at a last retail of $175, after more than 35 years of production. This particular example has a small firing crack, not easily noticeable, not likely to make the item vulnerable to damage, and not affecting value. Sculptor: Juan Huerta.

"Boy with Drum" (#4616 G/M), part of a series of musician kids retired in 1979. This example shows pinprick glaze pitting on the drum face, a minor defect rarely seen in Lladró, noted for its careful glaze application. Sculptor: Juan Huerta. $300–$350.

however, seen firing cracks in very vulnerable positions, such as the shoulder or elbow of a girl's arm, where the flaw was so long or so deep as to cause outright breakage if the item were tapped in just the wrong way. These are usually destroyed at the factory, but every once in awhile, one will slip through the quality-monitoring process.

A hairline fracture, by contrast, results from damage and is so called because it is often not much wider than a hair. These cracks will generally have a straight, tight-edged seam with no separation. Depending on how deep they go, hairlines are vulnerable to outright breakage.

Another kind of damage that collectors should avoid in Lladró is glaze crazing or crackling. In certain types of ceramics, crazing happens either deliberately in the manufacturing process or naturally with age. A good example is older Beswick figurines made in the UK, where it would be rare indeed to find one without surface crazing. But the manufacturing process and materials in a Lladró resist crazing, so it's fair to say that any Lladró figurine with a crazed surface has been heat damaged after initial sale (usually by being left too close to a heater or stove or having been through an actual building fire).

Damage and repair can sometimes be difficult to detect. Because Lladró has such delicate—and often tiny—projecting elements, anything found on the secondary market needs to be carefully inspected prior to purchase for chipping, cracking, and breakage. Vulnerable spots where damage may not be immediately evident without close inspection include the neckline, ankles and feet, and wrists and fingers of human models. Dealer string tags are often attached in a way that covers damage, so be sure to look under the string. Amateur repairs will often involve visible glue, and even the best glue repairs will fluoresce if you subject them to a blacklight.

A blacklight, handheld models of which are inexpensive to buy, can be a very useful tool for detecting some repairs, but it won't detect all damage. Repaired breaks may fluoresce, but chips usually won't. Also, other things besides glue will fluoresce under the light, including dust, greasy but easily removed substances, and some kinds of model paint. Finally, many restorers have become extremely skilled at what's called invisible restoration, in which the restored areas are neither visible to the naked eye (because porcelain slip is used to effect the repairs) nor visible even under blacklight. The only way to detect these high-end restorations is with an X-ray. (Some collecting physicians have been known to subject items to X-ray—to which their profession would give them ready access. Personally, and speaking as a serious collector in my own right, I wouldn't be that obsessive. Invisible to the eye *and* invisible under blacklight are plenty good enough for me to consider the item as whole.)

"In the Garden" (#5416 G/M) shows sculptor Antonio Ramos's talent for miniature detail. Purchased in an antique store, it was one of my first Lladró models. Before purchase, there were several places I inspected for damage: the girl's neck, her hands—and those little birds. $300–$325.

The calculation as to whether a damaged item is worth restoring depends, to some degree, on the availability of pristine examples of the same model and to the type of restoration in question. Restoration by a qualified artisan is quite expensive, and it will often be cheaper to buy a new example than to try to have the damaged one restored—again, assuming that pristine examples remain available. This is especially the case if part of a model is actually missing—say a hand or even a finger. Accessory part replacement (e.g., flowers or parasols) is a problem the manufacturer itself can sometimes help resolve by supplying the missing accessory, but when a portion of a molded item is missing, that's when the full artistic skills of the restorer must be brought to bear in actually reconstructing the missing part—and doing so in a manner that the repair is seamless and invisible. That sort of restoration takes a great deal of time and skill and is often supremely expensive.

Here's the formula for determining when to restore Lladró (or any other porcelain, for that matter):

Your acquisition price + restoration price = the amount you have invested in the piece.

Restored value = 75% of pristine value.

Restored value minus the amount you have invested in the piece = equity (net value of the restored piece).

Here's that "Nightingale" (#1226 G), one of Lladró's early bird models, sculpted by Antonio Ballester and retired in 1981, which I found in an antique store with a chipped bill—priced at $10 and a no-brainer for restoration.

If, at the end of the last equation, you have a positive equity value, then the restoration is probably worth doing. If you have a negative value, it probably isn't.

Let's apply this formula to a real-life example. I purchased, at an antique shop, a bird model, "Nightingale" (model #1226 G), which was retired in 1981 and is not that easy to find. Because the very tip of the bird's beak was missing, the dealer had marked it a mere $10. Buying it and attempting restoration seemed a no-brainer to me at that price, so I bought it and sent it immediately to my favorite restorer, Jody Leak of Leak Enterprises in Florida, for an invisible restoration. That cost me $90. In pristine condition, the model is worth about $300–$350. So let's plug these values into the formula and see if the restoration was worth doing:

$10 [acquisition price] + $90 [restoration cost] = $100 [total investment]

Restored value = 75% of $300 [taking the low end of the pristine value range] = $225

$225 restored value – [minus] $100 [the amount I have invested in the piece] = $125 [my remaining equity]

In this case, the restoration was worth doing because, even with a conservative pristine value estimate as the basis for the calculation, I still have, at least in theory, $125 of remaining equity in the piece (see photo on p. 54). It's also useful to ask the "compared to what" question here, the answer to which is paying a lot of money to get a pristine replacement; chances are slim, indeed, that I could buy an undamaged example for the $100 I have into this one!

The exceptions to the "75% rule" are genuinely rare or scarce pieces not otherwise available, condition and price notwithstanding, and flowerwork restoration. Depending on the quality of the restoration, a serious collector may well be willing to pay top dollar for a restored example of a rare item not likely to become available again on the secondary market in the collector's lifetime. As to flowerwork replacement, Lladró has, in the past, regarded professional restoration of its flowerwork by a qualified restorer and *using Lladró-supplied parts* as a restoration to pristine condition.

To apply this formula to another real-life example, let's use my decision to have the flowerwork restored on "Kittens in a Basket with Flowers" (model #1444), a model retired in 2005 but purchased on the secondary market when it was still available as a retail piece. I bought it, with some of the flowerwork damaged, for $255, as compared to a then-already-hefty retail price of $625, a price that would have been well beyond my means at the time.

I thought I might be able to live with the broken petals and leaves, but, as my personality would have it, the damage plagued me to do something about it every time I looked at the piece. Finally, I sent it to Jody Leak, after learning that the reapplication of the broken flower pieces, using Lladró-supplied parts, was going to cost me $170. (I had previously had her invisibly restore a rare Lladró with two complete breaks in it for only $200, which gives you an idea how expensive it is to repair flowerwork! This is understandable when we remember that the process of replacing it is the same as the process for applying it at the factory in the first place: petal by minuscule petal!)

Now let's plug numbers into the formula—bearing in mind that in this instance, the company regarded flowerwork restoration, using its parts, as being restoration to 100% (rather than just 75%) of pristine retail value:

$255 [acquisition] + $170 [restoration] = $425 [total investment]

Restored value = $625 [the then retail price, with 100% value restored]

$625 minus $425 = $200 [equity]

In other words, I saved $200 on the price of a pristine item by buying the item on the secondary market and having the flowerwork restored as opposed to buying it retail, so the restoration was worth doing. An additional advantage of this restoration, for a collector of modest means such as myself, was that the total outlay for acquiring what would eventually amount to a pristine model was spread over two payments (initial purchase and flower restoration) rather than being incurred all at once in a retail acquisition at a much-higher cost.

Unfortunately, recent word is that Lladró is no longer regularly supplying replacement parts, such as flower petals and leaves, to professional restorers. But you may still find a restorer who has a remaining inventory of spare decorative parts or who can still get them via a specific contact at Lladró.

It should be noted here that there is a continuum of restoration by qualified artisans. The repair can range from careful piecing together of broken parts, but with the breaks still showing, to a mend that is totally invisible except under X-ray. For purposes of the calculations above, I have assumed a 25% decrease in value for any restoration except flowerwork. But that may not always be the case for invisible restorations that are so skillfully done that, for all intents and purposes, the item is made whole. Invisible restoration should, of course, be declared on any resale of the item, but collectors will be far more willing to pay full value or close to it for an item invisibly restored than for an item visibly repaired.

FINDING REPUTABLE ACQUISITION SOURCES

Obviously, the safest and most reputable place to acquire retail Lladró used to be from an authorized dealer. However, as previously mentioned, that authorized network has retracted markedly so that it is mostly consolidated in large urban centers not readily accessible to most collectors. Besides, this is a book about retired Lladró and Lladró brand models, and that means it's no longer dealing with the retail market but, rather, the secondary (after retail) market, where the frontier is quite a lot wilder and more unregulated.

At least for now, recently retired models can sometimes still be purchased from the back inventory of the few authorized dealers remaining. For many of the oldest and most desirable models, however, there's no substitute, in guarantees and consumer protections, for buying from a reputable secondary-market broker, the most famous of which is A Retired Collection in Longboat Key, Florida. Owner Janet Hammer is ethical and trustworthy, and while it's generally quite a bit more expensive to buy an item from her than to buy it on the open market, serious collectors often prefer to buy from reputable brokers because they know they can trust the quality, condition, and authenticity of what they're buying. Janet, with her astonishing network of connections, is often the only game in town for locating rare and hard-to-find models—which is why most insurance companies accept her prices as insurance replacement values.

"Libra" (#6220 G), one of 12 zodiac figures with conical hats standing or sitting over a globe. Bought it at a discount department store, but the logo had not been removed. On the retail market only from 1995 to '97, with Virgo and Libra the most expensive now. Sculptor: Salvador Debón. $375–$400.

I've had very good luck finding Lladró in antique and consignment shops that carry high-end merchandise—and even antique shops that don't, but whose owners or dealers may find an odd Lladró here and there and either don't recognize what they have or simply aren't interested in it. Such sellers are often motivated to offer the item at a price far below its actual value. I once had a dealer nervously tell me he was desperate to move a lovely Lladró that I bought from him for a song: "Just get it out of here before I break it!" he said.

One advantage of buying Lladró from an antique store, show, or live auction is that you can physically inspect the item to be sure that it's authentic and undamaged. Reputable antique dealers will declare known damage. A few antique dealers, though, make it a matter of habit not to warn consumers about known damage, or they adopt an undeclared strategy of "pricing to reflect damage," making it difficult for the potential buyer to distinguish between a damaged item and one that is simply priced to move. Just as often, though, the dealer doesn't *see* the damage; most antique dealers are generalists, not porcelain specialists,

"Kittens in a Basket with Flowers" (a.k.a. "Purr-fect," model #1444 G), purchased on the secondary market with minor damage to flowerwork, then restored by Jody Leak of Leak Enterprises using Lladró-supplied flower parts. (I fear Lladró may no longer be supplying replacement parts to restorers.) Retired 2005. Sculptor: Juan Huerta. $650–$675.

"Girl with Calla Lilies" (model #4650 G/M), here shown in its matte version retired in 1991, was purchased at an antique mall. Hard to find with delicate lily flowerwork intact, it's just the thing I would never risk buying from an online auction. Sculptor: Vicente Martinez.

My parents were with me when I found "Nippon Lady" (model #5327 G). Seeing it, Dad exclaimed nervously, "Oh, the hands, the hands!" First issued in 1985 and retired in 2000 at a last retail price of $595. Sculptor: Salvador Debón. $650–$700.

Gres "Sincerity" (#2422), issued 2001, retired 2003 at a last retail of $575 USD. If you were to find this on the secondary market, you'd want to inspect the flowerwork carefully before making a decision to buy. Sculptor: Begoña Jauregui. Courtesy of Joëlle Ley.

Here's the matte "Girl with Bonnet" (a.k.a. "Girl with Hat"; #1147 G/M) I bought years ago for $18 at an antique shop, removable felt covering the mark. Part of a series of girls seated on hassocks, in various poses of playing adult dress-up, retired in 1985. Sculptor: Vicente Martinez. $200–$225.

and they're not necessarily looking at their inventory with a collector's eye. So unless you're buying from a broker who offers formal condition warranties and authenticity guarantees, there's no substitute for the buyer's own careful inspection of a secondary-market piece prior to purchase.

Often, Lladró offered on the open secondary market *is* damaged, which is why the original owner has divested of it. In particular, it's rare to see an item with flowerwork on the secondary market where the flowers aren't damaged. I predict that, a century or more hence, collectors will be much more tolerant of damage to Lladró flowerwork, just as collectors of eighteenth-century Meissen are of antique flower- and lacework today. But for Lladró, that time is not yet.

The fun of shopping on the secondary market is that one can often find some truly extraordinary deals. I once ventured into a local antique shop and found a Lladró matte-finish "Girl with Bonnet" (model #1147). It was on a shelf with a bunch of other knickknacks the shop owner had purchased from some estate somewhere. He had marked each of these items $18, his *price du jour* when he was tagging them. At the time, I wasn't as familiar with the Lladró corpus as I am now, but I had started collecting it and already had a good eye for it—had even, in fact, previously asked this particular dealer to be on the lookout for it on my behalf. I spotted this item from across the room, saying to myself as I approached it, "Gee, that looks an awful lot like a Lladró." I turned it over to find green felt attached to the base, but I quickly discovered it was the detachable sort. Peeling it back surreptitiously, I immediately saw the Lladró mark. I brought it nonchalantly to the checkout desk, saying, "I like her. She's cute."

The proprietor said, "Yeah, she is cute," then tipped her over and, seeing the felt, said, "No mark, though." I didn't feel obliged to enlighten him, especially

"Koala Love" (#5461 G), in production for only five years (1988–1993). I purchased it in 1997 from Janet Hammer at $225 on a last retail price of $115. Today, she prices it at $355. A later version of the model shows white variegation in the leaves. Sculptor: Antonio Ramos.

given my previous effort to educate him about Lladró, but paid his price and made a quick, though not unseemly, getaway before my barely repressed glee could give me away.

Many moons ago, I used to buy Lladró on eBay™ too. I stopped when it became clear to me, after a couple of unpleasant experiences, that there was just no effective way to guarantee condition when buying from (usually) amateur dealers who often don't even know what to look for in porcelain damage. In an online auction, buyers are at the mercy of seller descriptions of the merchandise, and these may not always be complete and accurate. It should also be noted that an item in pristine condition at the time of an online auction can too easily arrive in smithereens if the seller isn't skilled in properly packing delicate items for shipping. If you can make a couple of big scores, you might well consider it worth the risk. But if you want to avoid the hassle of returns and fighting for refunds on undeclared damage, it's best to rely on your own eyes and do most of your shopping on the ground rather than online unless you have a record of good experience with an online seller.

One used to be able to acquire recently retired Lladró at discount department stores such as Marshall's and TJ Maxx, which generally acquire their merchandise from the overstock or sluggish inventory of other retailers. Marks on these items had not been altered, and Lladró availability at these venues seemed to be regional and hit or miss. Not more than a handful of items would appear at any given time, usually in a locked case or at the jewelry counter, and there might be long dry spells between appearances. I learned to check in now and then, and a handful of items from my own collection have been purchased from these two stores. I suspect these few items also came from the authorized dealer pipeline, and the authorized dealer network having shrunk dramatically, it's been some years since I've been able to find Lladró in these particular retail venues.

HOW LIMITED IS A LIMITED EDITION?

Lladró has produced two kinds of limited editions: time limited and numbered. Time-limited editions are those produced for a specified and limited time, typically a year or less. These include annual Christmas issues, annual members-only pieces from the former Lladró Collectors Society, and the later Lladró Privilege models. In time-limited editions, the edition size or number is not on the base, and there is no way to tell how many were made and sold during the short retail life of the model. Numbered limited editions, on the other hand, have a specified edition size that can range from very small (under 100) to a few thousand. Each item from the numbered edition will have on the base its own number, sometimes over a slash and the full edition size, and collectors especially prize the lowest numbers in the edition sequence. Among producers of limited editions in high-end collectibles, #1 of a high-end limited edition is often reserved to company owners.

Most current manufacturers of what are today referred to as "collectibles" produce limited editions. Critics of the limited-edition phenomenon in contemporary collectibles point out that an edition size of 5,000 to 10,000 isn't really all that limited. The point is well taken. Some of Lladró's very earliest, nonlimited models were retired in the 1970s, well before Lladró's worldwide popularity hit its peak. Consequently, there would have been relatively few of them sold—certainly far less than the average numbered limited edition—making these very early models limited by default if not by intent. Likewise, an item on the market for only one or two years and then retired because of sluggish retail sales may have been made in fewer copies than an actual time-limited edition produced in just one year; somewhat perversely, such retail "sleepers" sometimes take off later on the secondary market, with demand far exceeding supply.

On the other hand, numbered limited editions (LEs) in Lladró are truly spectacular groupings, and not just the limited-edition "come-on" or marketing ploy that LEs may be for some other collectibles manufacturers. Actually, they are limited for the very practical reason that they are very large tableaux and very complicated to make. Because of limitations in warehouse space, Lladró generally makes its more complicated limited editions to individual order until the edition size is fully subscribed, and some of those (e.g., "Cinderella's Arrival" and "18th Century Coach") won't sell out until decades after the first numbers were produced.

Those in the best position to achieve value equity in a complicated limited edition will be those who bought older ones early in their production history. Limited editions that have been open for a long time and haven't yet sold out are now retailing at many thousands of dollars, leaving little room for later secondary-market appreciation. Another way to look at this is that for the retail price of a numbered limited edition today, one could amass an entire collection of older retired models whose production may well have been even more limited.

WHAT TO PAY

We can't always be lucky enough to find a "steal" on the secondary market, of course; sometimes we'll have to pay dearly in order to get a rare or highly desired model. This brings us to the question of what a collector should be willing to pay for a given retired Lladró.

It was somewhat easier to answer that question back in the halcyon collecting days of the early 1980s and 1990s, before the internet auction, when buyers were speculating like mad on Lladró's "investment potential" and driving secondary-market prices higher every year. Then, along came eBay™, and the collectibles market shifted rapidly and radically from a seller's to a buyer's market.

The effect of internet sales on Lladró prices was particularly depressive. eBay™ was the quintessential unauthorized retail conduit, and there wasn't a thing the Lladró company (or any other collectibles manufacturer, for that matter) could do about it. Instead of one copy of a current-issue retail model becoming available at sparsely located authorized dealerships or the occasional antique shop, several of that model were now being sold on eBay™ on any given day, with buyers able to take advantage of price competition and buy models for a small fraction of their authorized retail cost. If an unusual model came up for sale and happened to garner prices on eBay™ that approached the collecting prices of the 1980s, several more of the model would suddenly come out of the global woodwork from sellers hoping to achieve the same stellar price level—which, often, they did not. Collectors began to get a truer sense of actual production levels on scarce items; at least some Lladró items formerly thought to be rare began to surface on eBay™ with surprising frequency.

The eBay™ impact was particularly deflating for the value of annual pieces made exclusively for members of the now-defunct Lladró Collectors Society (LCS). There had long been considerable energy among members of the LCS to have a complete set of these annual issues, and eBay™ sellers attempting to capitalize on that need flooded online auctions with LCS figurines. This, of course, undercut the exclusivity of these figurines because they were no longer "members only."

"German Shepherd with Pup" (#4731 G), made from 1971 to 1975 and scarce since the company didn't then have capacity for large batches of a model. If you want it, you'll probably have to pay close to replacement value: $1,340 at A Retired Collection. Sculptor: Juan Huerta. Courtesy of Joëlle Ley.

"Flight of the Gazelles" (#1352 G) was a limited-edition grouping sold from 1978 to 1987 in an edition size of 1,500. (The catalog photo shows black striping on the underside of the lead gazelle, which may have been a later embellishment to the model.) Courtesy of José L. Gonzalez Rodriguez.

Base of "Flight of the Gazelles" with signatures of sculptors Vicente Martinez and José Ruiz, item number #557 (of a total edition of 1,500), and a "ghost" of redundant maker's mark that was probably removed at the factory. Janet Hammer lists the model at $5,450 (on a last retail of $2,450).

"It Wasn't Me!" (model #7672 G) from 1998 is an example of the time-limited edition that Lladró made annually for the Lladró Collectors Society (LCS). In making "members only" figurines available to all comers, internet auction sites undercut the "exclusive" aspect in their desirability. Estimated value: $300–$325. Sculptor: Antonio Ramos.

Issued in 1982 and retired in 1985, here's "Baby on Floor" (model #5101 G). Estimated value today: $200–$225—on a last retail price in 1984 of just $54! Sculptor: Salvador Debón.

Collectors began to see that rarity was relative as a seemingly endless supply of items in the LCS series were posted on eBay™ in any given week. Included were a surprising number of the very first issue in the series, "Little Pals" (#7600 G), a clown model with two puppies sticking out of his pockets. The value of this model had first been set by the live Lladró auctions held in Florida and California from 1989 to the early 1990s, where auction prices for it ranged from a low of $2,500 to a high of $4,500, although most brokers and other appraisal sources placed actual value at the lower end of that range. Nonetheless, by the late '90s, eBay™ prices for it were ranging in the low hundreds, and later LCS issues weren't going much higher than any other Lladró offered on eBay™. The LCS was later replaced by "Lladró Privilege," primarily a high-end marketing tool rather than a collector's society as traditionally understood. Privilege pieces don't seem to create the elite "buzz" among collectors that the LCS pieces did, and the program never really caught on.

There is a bright spot for collectors with large Lladró holdings and hoping not to see the equity they have in their collections swallowed up in the World Wide Web. Internet auctions have now been around long enough for people to experience the darker side of internet commerce. Seller misrepresentations of authenticity and condition, exorbitant shipping charges, damage resulting from poor shipping, and a famous scandal involving a dealer who advertised high-end Lladró inventory he didn't have and then absconded with several hundred thousand dollars in winning bidders' money have all dulled the attraction of internet auctions for acquiring Lladró.

COLLECTING— OR MERELY SPECULATING?

People have staked business lives and personal resources on Lladró's formerly legendary appreciation in market value. As with bubbles in the stock market, banking business, and real estate, many speculators had managed to convince themselves that the prices of Lladró would rise forever. In fact, reality was already beginning to assert itself as far back as the early 1990s in the Lladró secondary-market live auctions in Florida and California, when auction sponsors had difficulty getting collectors to part with items because auction estimates— not to mention actual gavel prices—did not, even then, match the inflated figures of their owners' dreams.

Using the price records from these special Lladró auctions as published in a now-defunct magazine called *A Work of Art*, I did a numbers analysis on this benchmark for secondary-market values, showing how auction trends changed from the earliest to the latest auctions. In their earliest years, when these auctions were just getting off the ground, collector interest in them was high. In 1989, 39.8% of the total auction lots failed to meet their preauction estimate range, but 21.3% of the total California auction lots sold above their auction estimate. In 1990, only 28.7% of total lots failed to meet the lower number in their auction estimate, and 19% sold above their auction estimate.[2] It was a healthy trend for sellers.

This set of three "Beagle Puppies" is among Lladró's most endearing animal creations. *Left to right*, "Beagle Puppy (#1071 G/M), "Beagle Puppy" (#1072 G/M), and "Beagle Puppy" (#1070 G/M). Estimated Value: $250–$275 ea. Sculptor: Julio Fernandez.

Fast forward to the California and Florida auctions in 1995. In the slightly smaller Florida auction, only 31% of lots failed to meet the lower number of their estimate range[3]—not much worse than the 1990 numbers, perhaps because A Retired Collection, Janet Hammer's well-respected and influential secondary-market brokerage, is located there. In California, on the other hand, a whopping 63% of consigned lots failed to meet the lower number in their auction estimate range. That year and in both auctions, fewer than 0.5% sold above their estimate range.[4]

Lest we draw from this data too rapid a conclusion about some sort of market slide in Lladró values, we should consider that the issue may, rather, have been excess optimism in the auction estimates. The factors that affect auction bidding are multiple and complex but include the understandable desire of buyers to pay as little as possible, which amounts to an incentive to bid and buy under the auction estimate. The vast majority of the lots that sold below estimate at these Lladró auctions still sold in the several hundreds of dollars.

During the investment fever seizing the Lladró secondary market in the early '90s, the Lladró company, to its great credit, publicly and consistently warned collectors against buying Lladró purely for its investment potential. Lladró is an untested investment option as viewed from a long-term perspective; during the specialized Lladró auction era, the company had been barely fifty years old. Some collectors still thought they were making a family investment, however, acquiring substantial collections they then intended to pass down to children who, as it turned out, didn't want them.

Today we understand much better that most models have a value plateau at which the top-end price levels out; the collector with the most equity in the piece

"Valencian Girl with Flowers" (#1304), issued 1974, when its issue price was a mere $200, a far cry from its $675 last retail in 2004. Sculptor: Juan Huerta. Courtesy of Teresa L. Schmitt.

will be the one who got in on the ground floor, when the retail price was lowest. Those who will have the most difficulty reaping their equity on resale will be those who bought an item late in its retail life or at the level of its price plateau on the secondary market (or both). Back in the 1960s and early '70s, models could be purchased at retail for under $20 that today trade on the secondary market for hundreds of dollars. That's an enormous value appreciation, even considering a dollar was worth more in the 1960s and '70s than it is today.

For example, Lladró made a set of three very endearing beagle puppy models (#s 1070–1072) back in the mid-1960s. At time of issue, you could buy these little rascals for $16.50 USD apiece! Their last retail price when they went off the retail market around 1990 was $135. By the mid-1990s, they were trading at $250 to $350 apiece on the secondary market. Except at well-respected brokerages such as A Retired Collection, that price range will be difficult to sustain, especially when the general economy is weak. Therefore, private collectors in the best "equity" position with these models will be those who bought them when they cost $16.50 each, and those who bought them at their last retail price won't be in bad shape either. Those who paid full price for them on the secondary market in the 1990s will, at least in the short term, be lucky to get their money back if they ever have to sell. (See photo on previous page.)

It should also be noted that Lladró, in what seems to be an effort to reap some of the benefits of value appreciation on especially popular retired issues, released two very similar models to these pups in 2014 with slightly different painting and perhaps just a bit smaller than the originals, but in essentially the same postures and both done by the same sculptor as the originals: #9134 "Sleeping Puppy" and #9135 "Playful Puppy," retailing at $200 each. These can be differentiated from the originals by the version of the mark and the impressed serial number on the base of the 2014 issues.

Another example of this "price plateau" phenomenon is "Valencian Girl with Flowers" (model #1304), a lushly decorated model in Valencia's colorful traditional dress and carrying a luscious bouquet of flowerwork. At its retirement in 2004, its last retail price was $675. The primary reason for a model retirement is, of course, when the model stops selling at the latest price. Looking at the length of time this model was on the market (thirty years!), we must first acknowledge that people were buying this model until it reached that last retail point. The end of a good run, in this case, appears to have been that price—and, atypically, A Retired Collection is today offering the model for $50 less than that last retail. From a purely financial point of view (and while acknowledging there's more to collecting than financial value), collectors with the best equity in this piece are those who bought it at its first retail price in 1974: just $200. Those in the worst equity position will be those who paid at or near its last retail price.

Despite its being a source of pride and prestige for the Lladrós, soaring secondary-market prices for retired models, such as the beagle puppies that Lladró had virtually given away in the early decades of the company's life, might well have rankled the manufacturer. A collectibles manufacturer, of course, gains nothing economically from a secondary-market sale. Consequently, Lladró has, in recent years, become much more adept, in its retail pricing strategy, at reaping future value up front. For many of the general-line models produced in the late 1990s onward, there is very little room for additional secondary-market appreciation above the original retail prices.[5] As an example, "Kittens in a Basket with Flowers" had already maxed out its value potential by the time it went off the market in 2005 at a last retail price of $695. As a result, Janet Hammer's A Retired Collection,

Stylized doves with early, impressed NAO marks, but all in a series of five also found with impressed Lladró marks. *Clockwise from rear:* model #s 62 G, 63 G, and 61 G. (missing: #s 59 and 60.) Sculptor: Fulgencio García. $50–$100 ea. for NAO marked; Lladró mark slightly higher.

whose prices are widely accepted in the insurance industry as replacement value, is currently offering the glazed version at that same retail price more than a decade after its retirement.

A particularly sensitive question is how much the values of items formerly thought to be extremely rare are affected by the discovery that some of these same models were made early on in other Lladró brands. In most cases, the production life was relatively short in whichever brand, and they were roughly contemporaneous in age, so while prices on Lladró-marked items that were formerly based on the assumption that the model was produced only in Lladró's core brand are difficult to justify today, at least some price premium may logically accrue to the same piece that is scarce in whatever Lladró brand. The truly ambiguous cases, however, are those in which old models of Lladró-marked items formerly thought to be essentially prototypical, and commanding secondary-market prices in four figures on the basis of that assumption, turn out not only to have been made in the NAO brand but, in some cases, to have been made in that brand for many years, with some retailing for less than $100 (see chapter 3 for more on this).

My bottom-line advice is to collect Lladró because you love it, not because you think you're going to be able to make a killing on it in some later resale. From this perspective, I'm willing, when I have the money, to pay a trusted broker top dollar for a model I really want and can't find otherwise. But when buying Lladró on the generic secondary market, I try not to pay more than a third to a half what I think it might be worth on some future day when circumstance might force me to sell it. I'm hoping, of course, that day never comes; I'd rather have my Lladró than the money! And that, my friends, is I guess what distinguishes a collector from a market speculator!

Opposite page

Top: "Dog in the Basket" (#1128 G), a whimsical model of a basset hound ensconced amid a bedspread in a laundry basket, was a gift from dear friends and is among my most treasured possessions. Issued 1971, retired 1985. Sculptor: Juan Huerta. $300–$350.

Bottom: "Bosom Buddies" (#6599 G), issued 1999, retired 2:02. Sculptor: Juan Huerta. $275–$300.

A
GALLERY
of Core Collection
LLADRÓ

"A Surprise Visit" (model #6409 G) and companion piece, "Will You Be Mine?" (#6410 G), both issued in 1997 and retired in 2000. Sculptor: Juan Ignacio Aliena. Courtesy of Teresa K. Schmitt. $200–$225 ea.

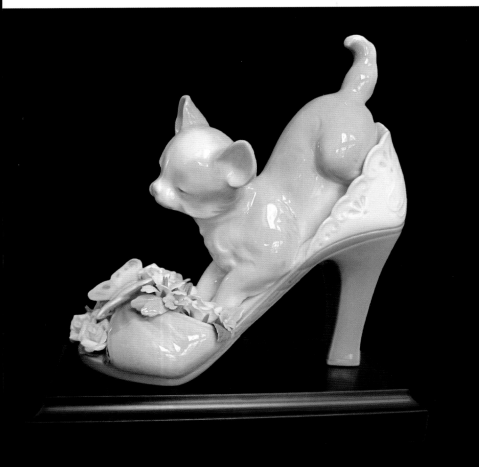

"A Cozy Fit" (#6743 G) and "A Purr-fect Fit" (#6775 G) issued in 2001, retired in 2004, two of several Lladró models of kittens and puppies in footwear and surrounded by flowerwork. Sculptor: Francisco Polope. Courtesy of Teresa K. Schmitt. Value: $300–$350 ea.

From left to right:
"Cat" (#5113 G/M), "Play with Me!" (#5112 G/M), and "Pet Me!" (a.k.a. "Surprised Cat," #5114 G/M), issued 1982. Matte versions retired in 1992, glazed 1999–2000 for "Pet Me!" and "Play with Me!" and 2010 for "Cat." Sculptor: Salvador Debón. $125–$150 ea.

Below:
"Scaredy Cat" (a.k.a. "Playful Kitten," #5091 G/M), both matte and glazed issued 1980 and retired 1998. Sculptor: Vicente Martinez. $150–$175.

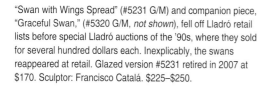

"Swan with Wings Spread" (#5231 G/M) and companion piece, "Graceful Swan," (#5320 G/M, *not shown*), fell off Lladró retail lists before special Lladró auctions of the '90s, where they sold for several hundred dollars each. Inexplicably, the swans reappeared at retail. Glazed version #5231 retired in 2007 at $170. Sculptor: Francisco Catalá. $225–$250.

"Skye Terrier" (#4643 G/M), first issued mid- to late 1960s. I managed to purchase this in 2007 for $50 (its last retail price in 1985!) from an antique dealer who normally charged exorbitant prices for Lladró but apparently didn't recognize the oldest backstamp as genuine. Sculptor: Salvador Furió. $300–$350.

Animal miniatures. *Back, left to right*: "Chihuahua" (#8367 G), 2009–2017, sculptor Juan Carlos Ferri Herrero; "Good Puppy" (#1289 G), 1974–1985 by Juan Huerta. *Front, left to right*: "Miniature Cocker Spaniel" (#5310 G), "Miniature Kitten" (#5307 G), and "Miniature Resting Dog" (#5309 G), sculptor Antonio Ramos, 1985–93. Estimated value: $150–$175 ea.

"Poodle" (#1259 G/M) was a gift from my late dad. Issued 1974, retired 1985 at a last issue price of just $65. It's a small model but can fetch big prices on the secondary market. Sculptor: Antonio Ballester. $350–$400.

Above:

Two more miniatures. *Left to right*, "Small Dog" (Papillon, #4749 G/M), 1971–98, sculptor Fulgencio García; "A Friend for Life" (#7685 G), issued in 2000 as a membership premium for Lladró Collectors Society, sculptor Juan Huerta. Estimated value of "Small Dog": $175–$200; for more rudimentarily modeled LCS poodle, $75–$100.

"Easter Bunnies" (#5902 G), issued 1992, retired 1996. Sculptor: José Luis Alvarez. Estimated value: $300–$325.

Caricatured "Donkey in Love" (a.k.a. "Donkey with Daisy," #4524 G/M) playing "She Loves Me" on a daisy, petal marked "NO" stuck to bottom of hoof, remaining petals arranged so no matter which way he goes, he'll end up on "SI." Smart donkey! Sculptor: Fulgencio García. Estimated Value: $325–$350 (intact example).

Large "Cow" (#1390 G) from Salvador Furió's classic Nativity set shown in chapter 1, retired in 2006. The style of Lladró Nativity animals is such that they can be displayed as stand-alone models in any season. $300–$325.

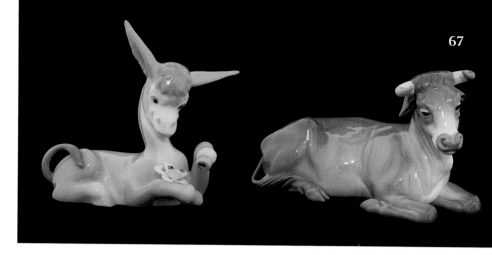

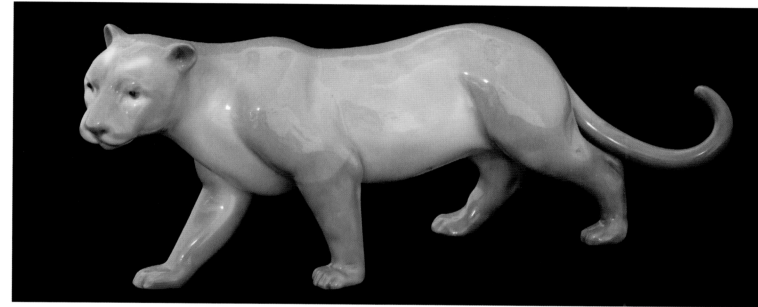

Above:

In addition to domestic animal miniatures, Lladró's Antonio Ramos also sculpted a number of wild-animal miniatures. "Miniature Cougar" (#5435 G) was issued in 1987 and retired in 1990. Lladró animal miniatures are popular but scarce and command prices out of all proportion to their size. $200–$250.

From a series of four, *left to right*: "Snack Time" (#5889 G), "Washing Up" (#5887 G), and "Hippity Hop" (#5886G). Missing: "That Tickles" (#5888 G), all issued 1992 and retired 1995. Sculptor: José Luis Alvarez. Estimated value: $125–$150.

"Miniature Seal Family" (#5318 G), issued 1985 and retired 1990, also sculpted by Antonio Ramos but a bit more pricey, perhaps because of the relative paucity of seal models in Lladró vs. polar bears as one of its favorite and frequent subjects. $225–$275.

Gres "Donkey Resting" (#2106), issued 1978 and retired 1983. Sculptor unknown. Courtesy of Joëlle Ley. Back ordered at A Retired Collection for $500.

"Polar Bear Miniature" (#5434 G), issued 1987 and retired in 2000. Sculptor: Antonio Ramos. $150–$175.

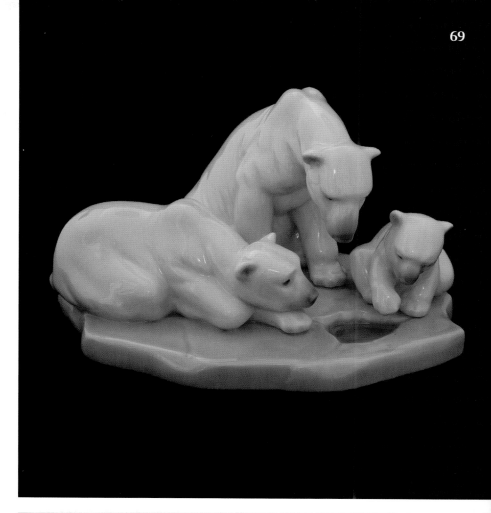

"Polar Bear Family" (a.k.a. "Bearly Love," model #1443 G/M). Given the threat of continual polar ice melt from warming seas, the curious cub pawing at a hole in the ice while its anxious parents look on seems especially poignant. Sculptor: Juan Huerta. $175–$200.

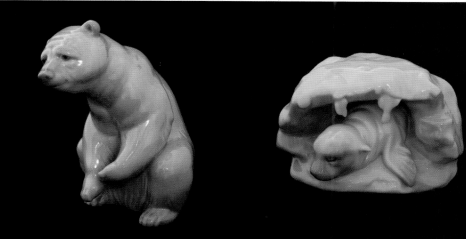

"Good Bear" (#1205 G/M) from a set of three brown bears, model clones of white polar bears still in production. Both sets were issued in 1972, but brown bears were retired in 1989, while polar bear set is still open. Sculptor: Juan Huerta. $150–$175 ea. (brown versions).

"Snowy Haven" (model #8061 G), a simple model issued in 2004 and off the market by 2008 at a last retail price of $170, with no discernible secondary-market appreciation, since the manufacturer, in its retail pricing strategy, seems inclined to reap future value up front. Sculptor: Antonio Ramos.

Among Lladró's special collections is its "Peaceable Kingdom Collection," based on Isaiah 11:6–9: "The wolf also shall dwell with the lamb . . . and a little child shall lead them." Here, "And the Leopard Shall Lie Down with the Kid" (#6926 G), retired in 2007 at $245.

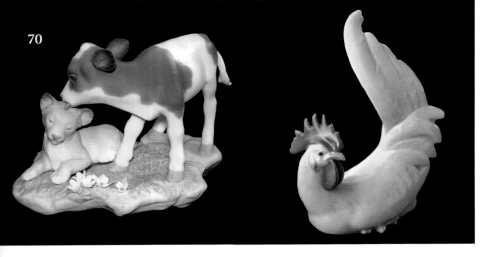

From Lladró's Peaceable Kingdom Collection, "And the Calf and the Young Lion" (#6927 G), retired also in 2007, retail price $245. Sculptor for this collection is Begoña Jauregui, one of only a handful of female sculptors at Lladró. Courtesy of Jorge L. Gonzalez Rodriguez.

"White Cockerel" (#4588 G/M) retailed from the late 1960s to 1979 at a last retail of just $50 (shoulda bought it then!). Sculptor: Alfredo Ruiz. Courtesy of Joëlle Ley. $375–$400.

"Ducks Group" (4549 G/M), issued 1960s, retired in 1991 for the matte and 1996 for glazed. (Note snail on the reed.) Ducks from this grouping were spun off as three individual models (#s 4551–4553) and are more often seen on the secondary market. Sculptor: Fulgencio García. $200–$250.

The three little ducks spun off as individual models from the larger grouping also shown here. *Clockwise from left*, #s 4551, 4552, and 4553. Sold individually and as a set (#7909). Matte versions retired 1991, glazed 2001. Sculptor: Fulgencio García. $50–$75 ea.

Matte version of "Moses" (model #5170 G/M) was retired in 1991 and the glazed (*shown here*) in 2000, last retailing at $410. Lladró has several models that depict Old Testament and Judaic themes. Collectors especially seek Lladró models of rabbis. Sculptor: Francisco Catalá. Courtesy of Jorge L. Gonzalez Rodriguez.

"Young Mary" in a Gres treatment (#2417) was issued in 2000 and retired in 2002 at a last retail price of $340. The model measures a little over a foot tall. Sculptor: Begoña Jauregui. $375–$400. Courtesy of Joëlle Ley.

"Angel Wondering" (#4962 G/M) is here shown in a matte finish, retired in 1991. The glazed version is still in production and retailing at $195. Sculptor: Salvador Debón.

"Angel Tree Topper (Pink)" (#5831 G), time-limited edition for 1993. Details such as the musical notation painted on the banner enhance the joy of Lladró collecting. (I wouldn't entrust this and similar angels to a treetop, but they work well as freestanding figurines.) Sculptor: Francisco Catalá. $175–$200.

"Angelic Cymbalist" (5876 G) tree topper, a time-limited edition in 1992. Sculptor: Joan Coderch. $175–$225.

"Heavenly Harpist" (#5830 G), time-limited edition for 1991. One of the delightful things about these angel tree toppers is the detail in the dresses, distinct for each, this one with a rose pattern and a different floral and vine decoration on the blue hem. Sculptor: Francisco Catalá. $225–$250.

"Rejoice" (#6321 G) was the time-limited tree topper for 1996. While most Lladró is attributed to a specific sculptor, every once in a while an item is attributed, as this model was, to the "Department of Decoration and Design." $225–$250.

Above:
"How Skillful" (#6517) is a winning Lladró combination of a pet cockatoo and a whole bunch of flowerwork, but last retail price of $440 was maybe a bit too rich since it was produced in a period of only five years, 1998 to 2004. Courtesy of Teresa K. Schmitt.

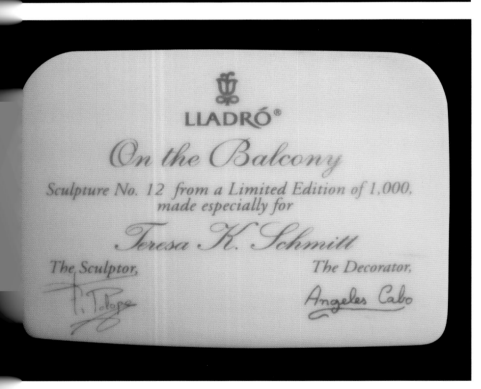

Top left:
A complicated limited edition that really shows Lladró's technical and aesthetic virtuosity, "On the Balcony" (#1826 G) was issued in 1998 in a limited edition of 1,000 and retired in 2002 at a last retail of $3,200. Sculptor: Francisco Polope, Courtesy of Teresa K. Schmitt.

Center:
In addition to the information on the base, Teresa has a special confirmation of the identity and authenticity of her limited edition in this porcelain plaque documenting it as only the 12th one made.

A close-up of the detail in Teresa's "On the Balcony." No wonder Lladró doesn't warehouse them but makes these complicated limited editions only to order!

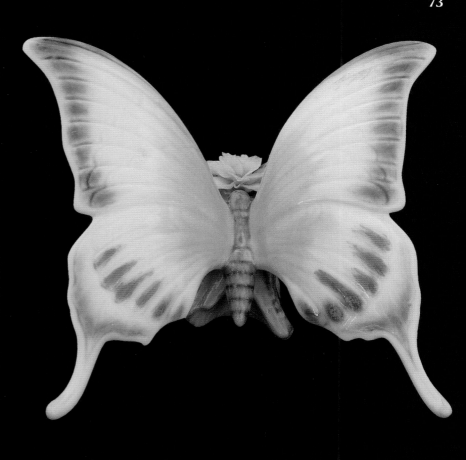

Above:
Issued in 1974, "Little Ducks after Mother" (#1307 G/M) had a long retail run in its glazed version, retiring in 2017 at $180, the matte having been part of that mass matte model retirement in 1991. Sculptor: Juan Huerta.

Right:
Lladró produced several models of butterflies perched on blossoms for the regular line or as special orders. "Spring Butterfly" (#7202 G) was made as an exclusive/limited issue for Gump's by Mail in 2002. Back in 1989, Lladró's Department of Decoration and Design also made delicate butterflies out of porcelain-fired lace. $175-200.

"Valencian Boy" (model #5395 G/M), issued 1986 and retired 1991. Its last retail price was already $325—and it hasn't gone down since. Estimated value: $375–$400. Sculptor: Antonio Ramos. Courtesy of Teresa K. Schmitt.

"Spanish Dance" (#6444 G), issued 1997 and retired in 2000 at $545, but you can add another $400 to its replacement value! Those arms and hands and a short production run would make pristine examples scarce. Sculptor: José Javier Malavia. Courtesy of Teresa K. Schmitt.

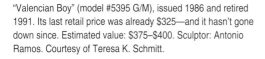

"Ceremonial Princess" (#6424 G), bought in 1997, was still its last retail price of $240 when it retired in 2000. The ways of the secondary market can be inscrutable; today, her replacement value at A Retired Collection is $550! Sculptor: Antonio Ramos.

Gres "Arctic Allies" (model #2227), issued in 1992 and retired in 2004 at a last retail price of $650. Sculptor: Juan Huerta. Courtesy of Joëlle Ley. $675–$750.

"Poor Little Bear" (Gres #2232) was sculpted by Juan Huerta, who seemed to have a particular attraction to indigenous northern cultures, since he made several models based on them, especially in Gres. Issued 1992, retired 2004 at a last retail of $285. Courtesy of Teresa K. Schmitt.

"Eskimo Boy and Girl" (Gres model #2038), issued in 1971 and retired in 1999 at a last retail of $595. Sculptor: Juan Huerta. Courtesy of Joëlle Ley. $650–$750.

"Pacific Beauty" (Gres #2403), issued 1999, retired 2001 at a last retail of $850. Sculptor: Alfredo Llorens. Relative scarcity of Gres on the US secondary market gives her added value on this side of the pond. Courtesy of Joëlle Ley. $1,100–$1,200.

"Caress and Rest" (#1246 G/M), issued 1972, retired 1989. Sculptor: Juan Huerta. $250–$300.

Below:
"Girl with Slippers" (#4523 G/M) and "Boy with Dog" (#4522 G/M) really need each other to form a narrative: girl calls dog to fetch slippers, boy cautions dog not to give itself away. Matte versions retired in 1991, glazed in 1997. Sculptor: Vicente Martinez. $100–$135 for #4523, $175–$200 for #4522.

Above left: "Boy from Madrid" (#4898 G/M), issued 1974 and retired 1997. Sculptor: Francisco Catalá. Estimated value: $175–$200.

Above middle: "Girl with Pig" (1011 G/M), here in matte retired in 1991, the glazed version retired in 2001, is a small figure spun off from a larger, uncataloged model in which she is surrounded by a herd of resting pigs. Sculptor: Fulgencio García. Single model $150–$175, grouping with pig herd $400–$450.

Above right: One of several "Girl with Lamb" studies in Lladró brands, this one the core collection's #1010 G/M, here in matte. The little girl's facial expression (see close-up in the introduction) is priceless. Sculptor: Julio Fernandez. $150–$200.

Right: The tallest of Lladró's "Girl with Lamb" models (#4584 G/M), its elongated style further exaggerated as she struggles to hold an adolescent lamb on her hip. Sculptor: Alfredo Ruiz. $175–$225.

"Shepherd" (#4659 G/M) leaning in an exaggerated posture against a tree trunk, border collie at his feet. Issued in the mid- to late 1960s, it was retired in 1985. Sculptor: Vicente Martinez. $275–$300.

Bottom left:
Two little clowns with pups; *left to right*, "Pierrot with Puppy" (#5277 G/M) and "Pierrot with Puppy and Ball" (#5278 G/M), companion pieces released in 1985 and retired in 2007. Sculptor: José Puche. $150–$175 ea.

Bottom right:
Lladró made two models, a boy and a girl, for each day of the week, on the basis of a traditional children's rhyme. Wednesday's child is said to be "full of woe," but Lladró's "Wednesday's Child" (#6016 G) "knows no woe" instead! Sculptor: Juan Huerta. $325–$350.

"Little Girl with Cat" (#1187 G/M), issued in 1972 and retired in 1989. Sculptor: Juan Huerta. $300–$325.

Below:
Wonderfully endearing, "Sweet Dreams" (#1535 G/M) is finely detailed right down to the embossed decoration all around the pillow, including the back of the model, where it would rarely be seen except in a 360-degree display space. It was issued in 1988 and retired in 2004. Sculptor: Antonio Ramos. $300–$325.

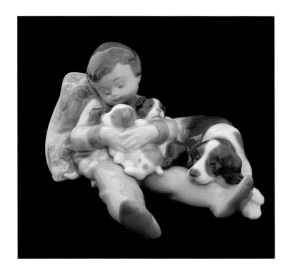

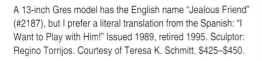

A 13-inch Gres model has the English name "Jealous Friend" (#2187), but I prefer a literal translation from the Spanish: "I Want to Play with Him!" Issued 1989, retired 1995. Sculptor: Regino Torrijos. Courtesy of Teresa K. Schmitt. $425–$450.

Gres "Repose" (#2169) was issued in 1987 and retired in 2004. Sculptor: Juan Huerta. The Gres formula lends itself to a rustic style with relatively few decorative details; the considerable charm in this model is in the lines of the sculpture. $200–$225.

"Girl with Cockerel" (#4591 G/M), here shown in matte, issued in 1974 and retired in 1991 (glazed just a couple of years later, in 1993). Sculptor: Fulgencio García. $200–$225.

"Feeding Time" (#1277 G/M), issued in 1974, retired in 1993. Behind her back, she holds a cone full of snails, a few of which she holds out in her hand. Ducks consider snails a great delicacy, so Lladró often includes them in its many duck tableaux. Sculptor: Juan Huerta.

Balanced on a skateboard, a precarious position only kittens could enjoy, "Little Riders" (#7623 G) was a Lladró "Event Figurine." These annual-event figurines were essentially a marketing opportunity for the company to sell figurines at their signing events, this one for 1994. Sculptor: Salvador Debón. $225–$250.

Below:
Gres model 2183, "Wake Up, Kitty!" issued 1989, retired 1993. Sculptor: Regino Torrijos. Courtesy of Teresa K. Schmitt. $350–$400.

Lladró also used the Gres formula to produce some gorgeous head busts, including "Gentle Moment" (#3564), a sold-out limited edition of 1,000 issued in 1994 and fully subscribed by 2002. Shown with framed limited-edition certificate. Sculptor: José Puche. Courtesy of Joëlle Ley. $2,500–$2,750.

"Corn for the Goose" (#1052 G/M) spares no detail, as seen in a close-up of the food kernels inside the bowl! Issued mid- to late 1960s, retired 1998. Sculptor: Vicente Martinez. $225–$275.

"Little Fisherman" in Gres, made 1993–99. Sculptor: Salvador Debón. Courtesy of Joëlle Ley. $325–$350.

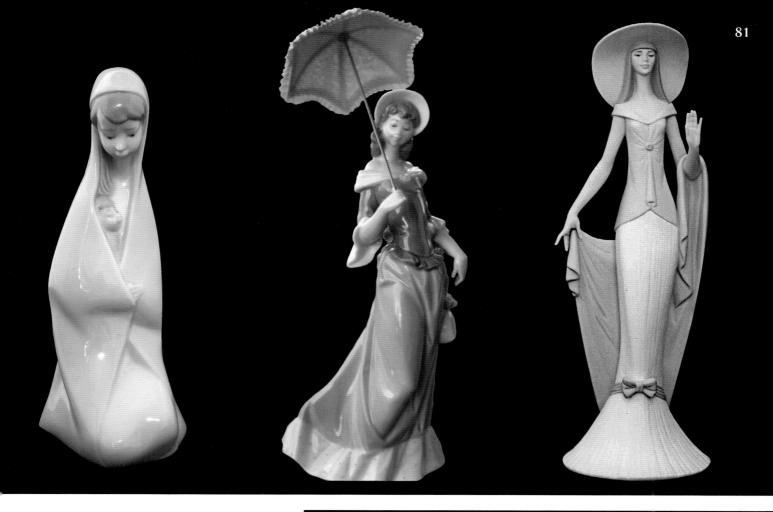

Above, left to right:

This simple model, "Girl with Child" (#4636 G/M), was issued sometime between 1965 and 1969 then retired 10 years later, just before US demand for Lladró heated up, making the model a limited edition for all practical secondary-market availability, which accounts for its value range. Sculptor: Juan Huerta. $250–$275.

"Walking" (#5003 G/M), issued 1978, retired 1993, with one of those lacy Lladró parasols. Sculptor: Salvador Debón. Courtesy of Joëlle Ley. $375–$400.

"Lady of Nice" (#6213 G/M) had a short production run, 1993–96. Sculptor: José Puche. At A Retired Collection, this scarcer matte version is offered at $610, about twice as much as for the glazed version. Courtesy of Teresa K. Schmitt.

One of my favorite Lladró models, "Little Girl with Turkeys" (#1180 G), issued in 1971, also had an early retirement date, 1981, before the collecting craze for Lladró took off in the US. Sculptor: Fulgencio García. $350–$400.

One of Lladró's larger groupings from the regular collection, "Feeding the Ducks" (#4849 G/M), issued 1973, retired 1995. Sculptor: Alfred Ruiz. $300–$325.

Fulgencio García's "Girl with Umbrella" (#4510 G/M), issued mid-1960s, although company sources give the year as 1969. (Umbrella originally applied with glue to the girl's hand so the accessory stood well above her head. Glue to apply heavy accessory elements was prone to failure.) Sculptor: Fulgencio García. $250–$300.

"A Visit to Dreamland" (#6786 G) was also on the retail market only briefly, 2001–2004. Last retail price was $500—owing in no small part to that large, broad flowerwork—and probably more than the retail market would bear. Sculptor: Francisco Polope. Courtesy of Teresa K. Schmitt.

Gres "Cat Nap" (#2320) retailed from 1995 to 1999, so a pretty short production run. Sculptor: Juan Huerta. Courtesy of Teresa K. Schmitt. $300–$325.

Another set of three ducks (#s 1263–1265 G), exceptionally well detailed in the feathering for models this small. Issued 1974 and retired 1998. Sculptor: Julio Fernandez.

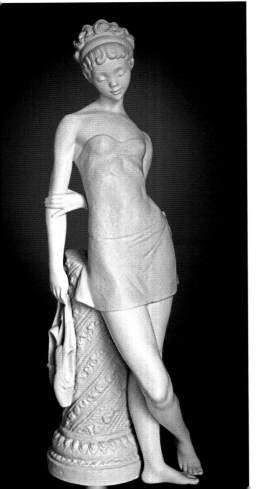

Left: "Dreams of a Ballerina" (#1889 M) is a simple but elegant and evocative limited edition of 1,000 that was available only in 2003 and 2004. The model is very tall at just under 22.5 inches. Sculptor José Puche. Courtesy of Joëlle Ley. $850–$875.

Above: While these may seem companion pieces, they were actually made at different times by different sculptors. *Front to back:* "Dove" (#1015 G/M), made from mid- to late 1960s to 1993 and sculpted by Fulgencio García, and "Restless Dove" (#6287 G), made only 1996 to 1998, sculpted by Francisco Catalá. $125–$150 ea.

CHAPTER 3

THE NAO BRAND

Early, uncataloged NAO goose with an impressed mark, among the happiest acquisitions from my few off eBay.™ Head, eyes, and feet are exquisitely modeled, one leg and foot separately articulated from the body; detail in the webbing and texture of the feet is phenomenal. Sculptor is unknown. $175–$250.

Close-up of the extraordinary modeling of the head in the uncataloged NAO goose. Note the detail around the eye and the nare (nostril) in the bill.

NAO (pronounced as in the English word "now") is the oldest of Lladró's alternate brands—and the only one still in production. Yet, it has been only in quite recent years that collectors have been aware of it at all. Once its connection to Lladró began to be more widely known, the NAO brand did not have the dampening effect on Lladró collector enthusiasm that, judging from its early efforts to obscure the connection, the company seems to have feared. On the contrary, many serious collectors have embraced NAO as one more opportunity to indulge their passion for Lladró porcelain—and at a more affordable price. While it is true that a collector needs to be aesthetically discriminating about which NAO to collect, that is true of any collector and any art form, including the core Lladró brand. Learning to separate the artistically valuable from the mediocre is—whatever the maker or name—an essential part of prudent collecting.

HISTORY OF THE NAO BRAND

It is a challenge to come up with a coherent NAO brand history. Much of the confusion stems from contradictions in the brand's own marketing literature and in books the Lladró company has published to promote its core brand. Another source of confusion is inconsistent and divergent explanations given over the phone by company representatives who genuinely want to be helpful but who are providing what is usually just their best guess in response to collector questions. It's important to remember that the company did not keep early records of its production and often simply doesn't know the answers to historical questions.

In what I've come to think of as the "Adam's rib" theory, with NAO playing the part of Eve, the company has sometimes claimed that NAO evolved directly out of the core collection and was motivated by the Lladró brothers' altruistic desire to make fine porcelain available to a wider public. Other accounts said NAO evolved out of another now-defunct Lladró brand. José Lladró, for instance, writes that NAO evolved from Rosal (a brand discussed in chapter 6).[1] One page of the official NAO website says that Rosal, which the website dates from 1967, evolved into Zaphir, which then evolved into NAO.[2] Finding a model produced both in NAO and Zaphir brands, and knowing the Zaphir model was made first but not fully understanding the chronology of the two brands, it would have been an easy leap for Lladró's customer service and marketing staff to reach the inaccurate assumption that not just the model but the entire Zaphir brand predated NAO.

NAO model evidence does not support a chronology that makes Zaphir NAO's parent brand. NAO models were being produced years earlier than the Zaphir brand, which the NAO website dates from 1975 (about right for Zaphir but way too late for NAO). On another page, the NAO website dates NAO from 1968,[3] which I believe is too late, but even if 1968 were the accurate year for NAO's first appearance, it couldn't possibly have evolved from Zaphir. The discovery of identical clones of early models made both in the NAO and the core collection brands, with both sporting impressed or hand-etched marks, also undercuts the "Adam's rib" theory that NAO was "taken out of" the core collection.

At the Lladró USA branch, much of the confusion over brand relationships seems to stem from staff turnover. In any case, José Lladró makes it clear that in at least one instance, the Lladró brothers themselves wasted no energy correcting erroneous information about the company, letting people think what they would as long as it served their overall marketing purposes.[4]

As to the claim that Rosal begat NAO, Rosal was a brand that Lladró invented expressly to put a rogue competitor out of business (see chapter 6), and, in his memoir, José Lladró claims his company immediately retired the few models it had in the Rosal brand once that was done. So although it is possible that Rosal was the genesis of NAO, it would be inexplicable why and how the still very young manufacturing company with its then-limited capacity could have retired the Rosal brand only to resurrect it as an entirely separate brand in addition to the Lladró brand the company already had. Aside from that, the earliest Lladró models, which the *Authorized Reference Guide* dates from the late 1950s and early 1960s, have also been found with old, impressed NAO marks. So if the turf wars that gave rise to Rosal began in 1967, it would have to follow that NAO predated Rosal by a few years.

Company marketing literature has also advanced two different explanations for the NAO name. One retail catalog said that its stylized, almost Grecian letters were based on iconographic and ornamental elements taken from glazed tiles and pottery, such as those found on Paterna wares produced in the Valencia region in the fourteenth and fifteenth centuries (the period of the last Islamic dynasty in Spain, which had been under Islamic rule since the eighth century).[5] This explanation appears to have been a guess by company marketers reaching for an intelligent, if fanciful, explanation for the name that sounded good.

The more commonly offered explanation in company literature—and the more likely one, given the masted sailing ship chosen as the logo for the brand, plus the location of Valencia as a port city—is that the name comes from an old generic term for a masted Spanish cargo vessel. Perhaps the most famous example of a *nao* was Christopher Columbus's flagship *Santa Maria*, whose full and formal name was *La Nao Santa Maria*.

Two stylized cats among NAO's very earliest issues in the 1960s, retired in 1972. *Left to right*, "Cat, Head Up"(#9 G) and "Cat, Head Down" (#10 G). Impressed NAO marks, and long retired by the time a logo backstamp was developed for the brand. Sculptor unknown. $150–$175 ea.

"Eagle Owl" (#712 G), first made in Zaphir and later as NAO, which, in addition to its own original models, has served as the receptacle for salvageable models in discontinued lines. NAO version was retired in 2000 at a last retail price of $75. Sculptor: José Roig. $75–$125.

For many years, Lladró seemed reluctant to admit publicly even that it owns the NAO brand—perhaps initially fearing that such an admission would undermine its core brand's reputation for high-end exclusivity. Even after admitting the connection, NAO marketing literature continued to insist that there was no relationship, either between the two brands' production facilities or the artisans who worked on the respective brands. Lladró published, both in its Lladró Collectors Society magazine *Expressions*[6] and as a separate marketing brochure, a series of FAQs whose purpose was to "clarify" NAO's relationship to Lladró. This is one of the places where Lladró explicitly denies any connection (other than equal qualification) between the artisans who worked on NAO and those who work on the core Lladró brand.

Production evidence shows, however, that the relationship between the two brands has always been symbiotic and that many of the most famous names in Lladró sculpting worked on the NAO brand as well as the regular Lladró collection. Moreover, while there are some sculptors exclusively dedicated to the NAO brand, several others have continued to work in both brands right up to the present day (see the annotated list of Lladró sculptors in appendix 2).

NAO IDENTICAL TWINS OF CORE BRAND LLADRÓ

The myth of strict, historically grounded brand separation was actually debunked when collectors themselves began to find old, impressed-mark models of NAO that were identical, in every respect save the mark itself, to old items in the core brand. Conversely, the models in the core collection that were identified as "rare" by the manufacturer and that had decimal-point model numbers in the company's collector catalogs were found, in many cases, to have early identical twins in the NAO brand. Judging from the impressed marks used in both brand versions, these early models appear to be contemporaneous with one another; that is, dating from roughly the same era of production. With one exception involving a Rosal model (see chapter 6), all cases of such cloning had Fulgencio García listed as the sculptor. The extent of this cloning phenomenon became increasingly obvious as the internet enabled collectors around the world to communicate with one another.

In a partially complete, list-only NAO database compiled by the Lladró company and supplied to me several years ago by a Lladró USA staffer, what appear to be the cloned models of decimal-point serial numbers in the regular collection were identified in the NAO line with a whole number preceded by a capital *L* and a zero. With this database, supplemented by production evidence from old catalogs and actual models, we can safely construct a table of items that have been found with both brand marks (NAO and Lladró). The abbreviation "UNKN" in the table below means the model number is unknown. The *L* numbers given below are those supplied in the NAO database as received from Lladró USA; these numbers seem to have been used for early issues before NAO had whole serial numbers without the letter prefix. Curiously, the same *L*-prefix numbers appear in an early Lladró price list from 1970, where they are simply identified as "Lladró."

With regard to the "Cowboy Boot" in the list above, a total of nine of these shoes were made, as pictured in a 1970 Lladró retail catalog, and is it highly likely that all nine models can also be found with NAO marks. There was also an additional "Dove" in the series listed above that appears in early NAO catalogs (#59), and it is very likely that this one, too, would be found in a Lladró-marked version.

"Boy with Hood" (NAO #354 G), something of a departure for sculptor Salvador Furió, famous for his historical and literary figures. Retired in 1998 at a last retail price of $80. With few exceptions, sculptors who worked on Lladró's core collection also worked on NAO. $100–$125.

In the elongated style of old Lladró, this matte model has an impressed NAO mark but is an identical clone of the well-known Lladró model "Girl Student" (#4518). Same model, parent company, sculptor, and production era: a Lladró by any other name is still a Lladró. Sculptor: Fulgencio García. $350–$400.

NAME	NAO Model Number	LLADRÓ Model Number
Hunting Dog	L051	308.13
Rabbit Standing	L052	309.13
Rabbit Resting (Long Rabbit)	L053	352.13
Rabbit Scratching	L054	278.12
Rabbit Couple	L055	279.12
Girl with Candle	L064	4868
Cocker-Type Dog with Snail	L071	UNKN
Polar Bear Observing	L075	UNKN
Medieval Boot with Buckle	UNKN	UNKN
High Jester's Boot	UNKN	333.13
Low Jester's Boot	UNKN	UNKN
Woman's Buckle Shoe	UNKN	UNKN
Woman's High-Top Boot	UNKN	UNKN
Cowboy Boot	UNKN	332.13
Romantic Couple	UNKN	304.13
Greek Shepherd	UNKN	342.13
Greek Shepherdess	UNKN	343.13
Girl with Lamb	UNKN	4505
Shepherd with Goat	UNKN	4506
Boy with Lambs	UNKN	4509
Couple with Parasol	UNKN	4513
Diana	UNKN	4514
Boy Student	UNKN	4517
Girl Student	UNKN	4518
Flamenco Dancers	UNKN	4519
Girl with Cockerel	UNKN	4591
Small Floral Vase	UNKN	4710
Girl with Lantern	UNKN	4910
Girl with Goat	UNKN	4756
Girl with Goose and Dog	UNKN	4866
Seesaw	43	4867
Cranes	45	UNKN
Ostriches	46	297.13
Goose (Neck Up)	52	UNKN
Goose (Preening)	53	UNKN
Dog (Seated)	57	UNKN
Dog (Reclining)	58	UNKN
Dove	60	UNKN
Dove	61	UNKN
Dove	62	UNKN
Dove	63	UNKN
Girl with Candle	64	4868
Boy Kissing	65	4869
Boy Awakening	66	4870
Girl with Guitar	67	4871
Girl Stretching	68	4872
Girl with Goose	114	UNKN
Playing in the Park	128	UNKN

Items Found Both with NAO and with Regular LLADRÓ Marks

These are simply the known clones to date. It is likely that others will be discovered.

Lladró's famous set of "Kids in Nightshirts" was produced and sold both under regular collection and NAO brands—the only instance I know where models were actually featured in the retail catalogs of both brands, though not simultaneously. Some are matte and some glazed. About half of those pictured here have NAO marks, and half have regular collection marks.

Calls and emails to company staff from other collectors and myself about these identical twins have elicited the information that Lladró sometimes "test marketed" its early models in what the company conceived as two very distinct markets, one for the core brand and one for NAO. Producing a few copies of a model for each market with their respective brand marks served as a trial balloon to see in which brand the item would sell best. The test market that garnered the greatest number of sales was the brand in which the item was definitively issued. This is at least a more plausible explanation than those that imply NAO evolved from some other Lladró brand. It still begs the question of why, this early in its history, Lladró would have been running two brands simultaneously. But that is a contradiction that appears irresolvable, and, again, this may not involve deliberate obfuscation on the part of the Lladró company but may, rather, result from the vagaries of memory in the absence of early production records.

On the basis of model evidence that includes this cloning of very early, seminal Lladró models, I have come to the conclusion that NAO and Lladró were largely

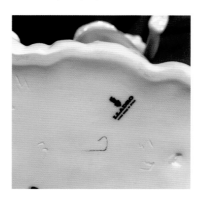

Lladró backstamp on what would become NAO's "Young Matador." NAO model retired in 1988. Finding an example with the first Lladró backstamp indicates the two brands were contemporaneous as early as the 1970s; even older impressed marks in both brands may push that dating back a decade.

Here's NAO model #161 G/M, "Young Matador"—except this one is marked Lladró. A model like this lends some credence to the theory that models were simultaneously test marketed to see which brand was the most lucrative retail home for general retail deployment. Courtesy of Brad Welch.

contemporaneous in origin, whether or not the Lladró brothers initially owned both. Further circumstantial evidence for this admittedly unproven hypothesis is the discovery of an early NAO "Marie Antoinette" model with an impressed mark in which the woman's costume is heavily accented by porcelain dipped lace, a technique used in the very earliest (ca. 1950s) uncataloged Lladró models, but not thereafter because of the extreme fragility of this Dresden-style decorative technique.

CHARACTERISTICS OF THE NAO BRAND

It was the startling similarity, both in theme and technique, that first led me to suspect that NAO was a Lladró brand even though the earliest marks didn't identify it as such and even though Lladró wasn't yet admitting as much. My very first NAO acquisition was a matte version of the astonishingly long-necked "Goose" (NAO model #52), which sported an older impressed NAO mark and which I bought because I loved it. At that point, I'd never heard of the NAO brand. I was very much a novice at Lladró collecting, yet I was unshakably convinced, from the first moment I laid eyes on this goose in a local antique store, that it was a Lladró. And I remained convinced even after another, more veteran collector had pronounced it "a fake." These many years later, I'm grateful that I followed my own instinct. Today, I continually enjoy and admire this piece for its technical virtuosity (that incredibly delicate and elongated neck!) and its simple, graceful beauty. If I had to divest of my entire Lladró collection of what is now a few hundred items and could only keep five to ten pieces, this NAO goose would be one of them.

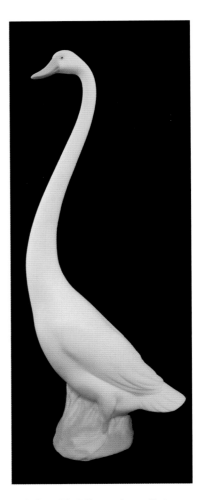

NAO "Goose" (#52 M), one of my earliest Lladró acquisitions, which collectors with more experience assured me was fake. Luckily, I listened to my own instincts. It has an impressed mark, but the glazed version was in production until 2001 at a last retail price of $60. Sculptor: Fulgencio García. I wouldn't sell it at any price.

Left to right, "Goose Reduced" (#54/2 G) and the larger "Goose" (#52 M), showing their relative size. The reduced versions of the two geese were retired in 1991. Those extraordinarily slender and elongated necks will make intact versions difficult to find on the secondary market. $150–$175 in either size.

"Boy, Big Hat" (#182 M) gets all the details right: a hat so big it nearly obscures his face, belly poking out over a waistband held up with rope, feet bare. Glazed version retired in 1996. Sculptor: Francisco Catalá. $150–$175 for the matte, $125–$150 for the glazed.

One of the characteristics of the NAO brand is sometimes said to be simpler detailing—simplicity, as exemplified by this model and a companion piece also called "Goose" (NAO #53) with its looping neck as the bird preens, being not at all incompatible with elegance. The basic modeling on these geese, which were also made in a size reduced by about one-third (model #s 54 and 55, respectively), remains anatomically bold, with the basic muscle contours well defined even though the feathering is not articulated in the stylized elongation of the basic shape. These two models have also been found with old, impressed Lladró marks.

Particularly in the early models (those produced through the 1980s), the same sculptors worked on NAO as worked on Lladró's core collection, and it seems to have been difficult for them to suppress their own instincts for embellishment in order to produce a "simpler" model for a lower retail price point. For example, "My Swan" (NAO model #1008), first issued in 1987 and retired in 1998, was developed by Lladró sculptor Vicente Martinez, who is noted for his attention to detail. This model certainly expresses that penchant for enhancement, from the ruffles and bodice detail in the girl's dress to the pinning in the swan's feathers.

Right:
Despite NAO's reputation for simplicity, no detail is omitted in "My Swan" (#1008 G), from the ruffles and folds in the girl's dress to the pinning in the bird's feathers. First issued in 1987, it was retired in 1998, last retail price $140. Sculptor: Vicente Martinez. $150–$175.

At first glance, there is little thematically to distinguish the models in the NAO brand from models in the regular Lladró collection. In NAO, we still find animal and bird models, models of children, ballerinas, harlequins, and elegant ladies, all favorite Lladró subjects. However, there are few "special collections" in NAO, and certainly nothing to compare with those in the regular Lladró brand—for example, no NAO equivalents of the Goyescas or the Klimt Collection or the Gaudí Collection. There are no "dark" themes in NAO such as found in the core Lladró brand. NAO's models seem heavily weighted to animals, birds, and childhood themes. Adult male models, relatively sparse in the regular brand, are even scarcer in the NAO brand, especially in recent decades.

For types of finish, the "big three" from the main Lladró line are also found in NAO: glazed, matte, and Gres. As a means of steadily reducing the expense and complexity of producing the NAO line, all its matte and Gres versions were eventually withdrawn from production (the matte in 1991, the same year the core Lladró brand also underwent a mass retirement of matte models, and the Gres in 2001). Because Gres models were more expensive to make, the price of a NAO Gres fairly well matched the price points in the regular Lladró line, thereby undercutting the retail rationale for NAO as a lower-priced alternative. More recently, NAO has started producing select Gres models again—still at prices that rival those in the regular Lladró brand.

One feature distinguishing NAO from the regular Lladró line is that NAO uses much less applied flowerwork. It will be recalled from the previous chapters that flowerwork, labor intensive as it is, serves to drive the retail price up. As with Gres models, use of flowerwork tended to defeat Lladró's retail strategy of offering NAO at lower price points on the retail market. Consequently, flowers in NAO are, with few exceptions, molded right into the model itself.

In something of a self-fulfilling prophecy, the NAO brand went through a patch, in the few years around 2005, where it seemed to have devolved in artistic quality. The few "special collections" that came out in the NAO line at that time are done in a cartoonish format and are, frankly, not up to the aesthetic standard previously set by the brand. (There is, apparently, a market for implausibly "cutesy" beings of this kind, of which the "Cheeky Cherubs" are a notable example; Lladró seems to have found a certain marketing niche with this series, since it has remained in production.)

But the NAO brand has come out the other side of the past decade with its artistic integrity intact. Older sculptors such as Francisco Polope and José Puche have continued to uphold the standard, and newer NAO sculptors such as Eva Maria Cuerva and Javier Santes are producing fine work that Lladró collectors would be proud to include in their own collections.

FOR COLLECTORS, WHY NAO?

Why *do* Lladró collectors collect NAO—despite the past efforts of the manufacturer to discourage its collectibility? As a starting point, the fact that Lladró owns the brand is significant for collectors. The brand benefits from the halo effect of that association.

Veteran collectors have also seen NAO as a source of expanded collecting possibilities, since, with the exception of early cloning, models made in the NAO collection were not made in the regular Lladró line. These collectors are capable of making sophisticated discernments about their Lladró purchases and, in either brand, collect only models that meet their aesthetic standards.

Price considerations are also a factor, particularly for collectors of modest means, who have seen retail prices of core collection Lladró rise in recent years beyond the means of Lladró's traditional collector base, for whom the most desirable secondary-market Lladró is sometimes also out of reach. Many antique dealers, even those with little knowledge of it, recognize the Lladró name. But they don't always recognize the semilegible impressed marks on older models,

Girls in similar posture and clothing, holding everything from roses to a duck to a rabbit or lamb, are marked either as Lladró or NAO. Here is an uncataloged, early, impressed-mark NAO holding roses. Where similar models have been attributed, sculptor was Fulgencio García. $75–$125.

"Lamb in Arms" (a.k.a. "Pet Lamb"), NAO #120 G/M, here in glaze. Although the company attributes Salvador Furió as sculptor, I've considered this a possible error—although fellow collector Jorge L. Gonzalez Rodriguez, who's partial to this sculptor, can see some elements he associates with Furió's style. $125–$150.

"Little Boy Blue" (a.k.a. "Little Shepherd," #521 G/M) retired in 1990. Although they were not made as such, this makes a nice companion piece for "Lamb in Arms" (#120 G). Sculptor unknown. $100–$125.

This impressed NAO-marked model, "Shepherd Boy with Goat" (#37 GM), is an identical clone for Lladró #4506 retired in 1985. The model is popular with collectors, and its NAO twin just offers a slightly greater chance of finding it. Sculptor: Fulgencio García. $250–$275 either mark.

particularly for the NAO brand, and some secondary-market sellers still aren't even aware that NAO is a Lladró brand. That means NAO can still be found at very affordable prices in places such as antique and consignment shops.

This is especially important when we consider the relative affordability of identical NAO versions of very early core collection models, whose scarcity with the Lladró mark can still command four-digit prices despite eBay™ and despite cyclically recurring economic recession. The discovery that some of these models can be found with old, impressed NAO marks has been of particular interest to discerning collectors who can't afford to spend a thousand dollars or more on a rare model with a Lladró core brand mark. Because the secondary marketplace hasn't really known what to do with these NAO clones, they can be surprisingly affordable even for people of modest means. In such cases, collectors find they can get not only the "look" they love but even some of the exact models they love without paying core collection prices for them.

Given the relative scarcity of these cloned models in either brand, I expect them to continue to command a price premium. Eventually, I believe the market will bring the respective values of these twins into closer alignment with one another. When something is made in identical models in two brands owned by the same company, made of the same precious material (i.e., fine porcelain) and modeled by the same artist-sculptor, it seems to me a case can be made that (to paraphrase Gertrude Stein's reflection on a rose), a Lladró is a Lladró is a Lladró.

Retail availability is another factor in NAO's collectibility. Collectors who used to have direct access to authorized dealers for new core collection issues now no longer have that access; the former network of authorized dealers has shrunk drastically to accommodate Lladró's strategy of consolidating its retail operations in the luxury areas of large cities and on real estate the company itself owns. At least in the US, this has made core collection Lladró less available to "average" collectors dispersed throughout the country who aren't that fond of internet commerce but can't just hop a private plane to New York City or Beverly Hills on a shopping junket either. NAO, by contrast, still maintains a less tightly controlled network of authorized sales. These factors have, in turn, affected the open secondary market: less core collection Lladró available locally and more NAO available instead.

Finally, the manufacturer's ambivalence toward the brand has lent NAO a certain mystique that—somewhat counterintuitively—has made the brand more, rather than less, attractive to many collectors. The gaps in its early-model chronology and the relative unavailability either of old retail or collector catalogs mean that retired NAO models previously unknown to most collectors are constantly being discovered.

Left, "Wake Up" (NAO #385 G), and *right*, "Tireless Puppies" (NAO #386 G), capturing the evolving postures, from sleepy to active, of these two cocker pups. Sculptor: José Roig. $150–$175 ea.

COLLECTING CONSIDERATIONS
AND CAVEATS

One of the signs that NAO has "arrived" as a desirable collectible is that it, like its core brand counterpart, has begun attracting the attention of counterfeiters. The few spurious NAO marks that have been found on the secondary market bear little relationship to authentic marks (unlike counterfeits of the core collection, where forgers at least *try* to make the mark look like the real thing), and NAO counterfeits are quite obviously inferior in quality to items produced in the genuine NAO brand.

As to condition, I would generally not recommend that anyone knowingly purchase a damaged NAO. As with the core collection, when a NAO model is extremely old and rare and unlikely to become available again in pristine condition, a knowledgeable collector might well want to have the item invisibly restored. But for more-common items, the lower retail price points for NAO, which in turn provide the floor for the secondary market, mean that restoration is very likely to cost more than the restored item would be worth.

As noted in chapter 2, seconds are a way for manufacturers of luxury products to recoup some of the costs of production on model copies that don't work out. Apparently, most NAO price points aren't high enough to justify the manufacturer's effort to market seconds in this brand—which is actually great news for serious collectors. Likewise, there doesn't seem to be any discount outlet or gray-market tampering with the NAO mark.

Shepherd with dog and lambs (NAO #38 G), with unusual first backstamp in cobalt blue rather than dark brown. I bought it despite damage (see neck repair) only because it was paired at a very inexpensive price with another model in pristine condition. Sculptor unknown, probably Fulgencio García. $200–$225 (pristine example).

 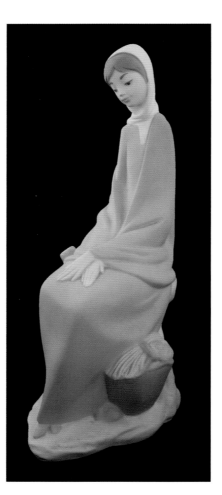

Left:
Shepherdess with herd of pigs (model # unknown but probably in the 30s as per related models produced at the same time), found in pristine condition and sold as a package deal with the damaged shepherd. Acquisition price for the two: $69. Sculptor: Fulgencio García.

Right:
In its core brand and NAO, Lladró often spun off separate figurines from more-complex models, as here in "Shepherdess" (NAO #37M), doing the same also with the shepherd from the model with dog and lambs. The model titles make more sense with the animals than without. $75–$100.

WHAT TO PAY

Four delightfully whimsical NAO white ducks, *clockwise from left*: "Little Duck" (#242 G), "Duck Looking Back" (243 G), "Optimistic Duck" (#245 G), and "Suspicious Duck" (#244 G). Made in matte (all retired 1991) and glazed (retired separately in years 2007–2012). Sculptor for the series: José Roig. $50–$75 ea.

As noted previously in this chapter, there are some great secondary-market bargains to be found in NAO models, especially when offered by sellers unfamiliar with the brand. However, the opposite is also true. Some secondary-market dealers know just enough about NAO to know it's made by Lladró, but not enough to know that not every Lladró is worth a king's ransom. This means they will sometimes overprice common NAO items that are still in production. Small individual models of ducks, for example, happen to be a favorite Lladró theme, and a series of four ducks with whimsical expressions on their faces are NAO's contribution to that tradition (model #s 242–245). All of these are now retired, the last two not until 2012—meaning that they were produced for a long time and that there is theoretically enough potential supply to meet secondary-market demand. Still, these ducks are sometimes found on the open secondary market priced well above their last retail price.

Determining specific issue and retirement dates on NAO is a particularly challenging enterprise because the company doesn't include retirement dates on the NAO website, and the web catalog uses a date in the 1990s as "year 1," much as the core collection catalogs use 1969 as "year 1" for that brand. So to determine retirement years for specific models, a researcher like me has to rely on access to retail catalogs and note the year in which any given model falls out of listing in those catalogs—or, alternatively, the year the model transitions on the official NAO website (www.naoporcelain.com) from the current retail catalog to the historical catalog.

Because of the historical ambiguity surrounding this brand and the ambivalence of its manufacturer, NAO is even riskier as an "investment" than is the core Lladró brand. The best advice I can give to NAO collectors is to buy a model because they love it, not because they expect it to double or triple in value during their lifetime. It follows that, with few exceptions, they would not want to pay big prices for retired NAO models. Those exceptions would, of course, include scarce or especially well-made models that one would be unlikely to acquire in any other manner except at this time, this place, and this price. The exceptions aside, find out what the last retail price was on the model, or make an informed estimate of what that might have been on the basis of what you know of other similar models, and try not to pay above last retail when buying on the secondary market.

Below:
Two of my favorite NAO models, *left to right*: "Dozing Doggie" (#1406 G) and "Comfy Kitty" (1407 G), issued in 2001, retired around 2008. Note the detail: weave in baskets, cable stitching in afghans, strands in yarn balls. Originally sold through QVC. Sculptor: José Santaeulalia. $100–$125 ea.

The oldest retired NAO models tend to be the best and the most valuable because they have strong aesthetic appeal, share the greatest stylistic affinity with the regular Lladró brand, and are sought after by other Lladró collectors. If you're going to collect NAO, this is where you would be best advised to concentrate your resources. Do, however, also keep an eye out for the work of newer sculptors, such as Cuerva and Santes, who are producing the high-quality current issues that will be the next wave of desirable retired models.

A NAO GALLERY

This large model, "Sweet Thought
enamel and matte variant of "Yout
was wearing a blue dress. The add
unusual in NAO. Sculptor: José Pu
$225–$250.

Another early NAO: "Ducks Group" (#6; right: matte retired in 1991,
and *left*: glazed, still in production and retailing at $59), a miniature
echo of the ducks grouping from the core collection (see Lladró
Gallery after chapter 2), except ducks are ogling a caterpillar
instead of a snail. Sculptor: Juan Huerta.

"In the Forest" (NAO #92G) has no further identifying information in the NAO brand's online catalog, but the elongated style is classical Fulgencio García. Etched NAO mark. $100–$125.

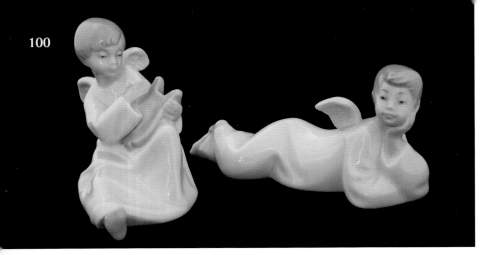

"Angel with Lyre" (NAO #14 G) and "Angel Reclining" (#13 G), NAO's miniature answer to the famous "child angels" in the regular Lladró collection. Very low model numbers place them among the first NAO, though they retired in 1990–91. Series had six angels (#s 10–15 G). Sculptor: Fulgencio García. $35–$50 ea.

Above: "Attentive Ballet" (NAO #146 G), last retail price in 2000 of $95. Ballerinas were a favorite Lladró theme and make several appearances both in NAO and the core Lladró collection. Sculptor: Vicente Martinez.

One of NAO's most endearing models, "Holding Her Puppy" (NAO #171 G, a.k.a. "My Pet"), was retired in 1997 at a last retail price of $135. Sculptor: Francisco Catalá. $175–$200.

"Man's Best Friend" (NAO #32 G), a large model in Lladró's classically elongated form. The boy appears to be wearing a yarmulke. The model was not only an early issue but also a relatively early retirement in 1984. Sculptor: Fulgencio García. $175–$200.

"Litter of Kittens" (NAO #104), in matte and glaze, was retired in 1990. Matte emphasizes modeling detail; glaze makes the colors pop. Love the vaguely exasperated look on the girl's face, as if it isn't the first time she's had to retrieve these kittens. Sculptor: José Roig. $125–$150.

Tall (11 inch) "Shepherd on Stile" (NAO #177 G), an early retirement in 1984. This example has NAO's first backstamp superimposed over another scraped-off, dark-colored mark—probably an original core collection mark, further evidence of the symbiosis between the two brands. Sculptor: Antonio Ruiz. $200–$225.

Speaking of earliest models, the serial number on this is 3! "Girl with Rabbit" (#3 G/M), here shown in matte. Matte version retired in 1991 and glazed in 1998 at $55 last retail. Sculptor: Fulgencio García. $100–$125.

"Traveling Girl" (NAO #1038 G) was a bring-over from the first year Golden Memories brand (see chapter 5) when the latter ceased production. It was retired from the NAO brand in 2008 at a last retail price of $85. Sculptor: Antonio Ramos.

Miniature grouping "Hen with Chicks" (#1047 G) was retired in 2001. Sculptor: Antonio Ramos. $50–$75.

Right:
The "Goose" in matte (NAO #52, *right*) was shown earlier in the book, but I wanted to show it here with its companion piece, "Goose" (#53, *left*), this one in glaze. Sculptor: Fulgencio García. Estimated value (for items unlikely to be found intact on the secondary market!): $150–$175 ea.

Left:
One of my favorite NAO models, "Swan" (NAO #107 G), was first issued very early, judging from the impressed NAO mark *and* what looks like an original impressed Lladró mark as well! Full-on NAO version wasn't retired until 2009–10 at $75 last retail. Sculptor: Antonio Ruiz. Value of dual-marked example undetermined.

Clockwise from left, "Attentive Duck" (NAO #370 G/M), "Two Ducklings" (#368 G/M), and "Little Duck Looking Back" (#369 G/M), shown in glaze. Love the baby wings! Matte versions retired 1991; all glazed retired 2010 to 2012, last retail $35 for the singles and $40 for dual model. Sculptor: José Roig. $35–$50 ea.

Left, "My Little Chickadee" (#372 G), and "Just Hatched" (#373 G) were early retirements, 1986. A rare case of the color being integrated right into the porcelain slip, a pale yellow instead of the usual white porcelain painted the desired color. Sculptor: José Roig. $35–$45 ea.

NAO made several stylized miniature animals, of which this "Miniature Owl" (#445 G) is the most commonly seen on the secondary market. It wasn't on the retail market long: 1986–90. Sculptor unknown. $35–$50.

Another uncataloged model, a cat with ball and wearing bow at base of tail, in the style of NAO #s 8 and 10, shown earlier in the chapter (but too much larger than they to be the missing model #9). Impressed mark, made ca. 1965. Sculptor unknown. $75–$125.

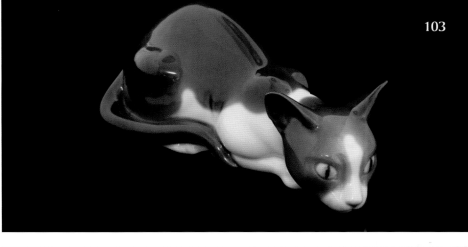

One of my favorite NAO models is this uncataloged NAO crouching cat, strongly reminiscent of a much-larger core collection Gres model (Lladró #2001) in same posture. Estimated production era: 1960–65. Impressed NAO mark. Sculptor: probably Juan Huerta, sculptor of record for the Gres Cat. $250–$300.

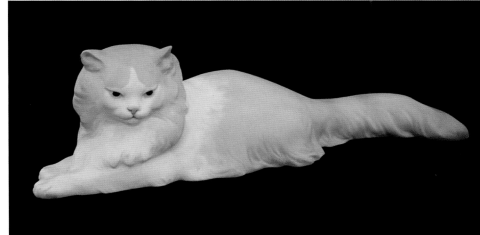

The matte version of "Angora Cat" (#113 G/M) was retired in 1991, then glazed in 2004 at a last retail price of $60. Perhaps because of the popularity of cat models, this is surprisingly scarce on the secondary market. Sculptor: Fulgencio García. Estimated value: $150–$175.

Left:
"Cat Playing on the Floor" (NAO #259 G), retired in 2000, had a companion piece, "Kitten with Yarn Ball" (#257 G), with the same cat lying on its side holding the blue yarn ball (retired 1990). Last retail price on #259 was $85. Sculptor: José Roig. $100–$125.

Right:
One of NAO's finest models, "Proud Cat" (#254 G/M) has been off the retail market a long time, the matte retired in 1984 and the glazed in 1990. Sculptor: José Roig. $150–$175.

"Collared" (#491G/M) and looking none too happy about it! Made in matte and glaze, both versions were retired in 1991. Sculptor: José Roig: $75–$95.

"All Decked Out" (#492 G/M), matte retired in 1991, glazed 10 years later at a last retail of $80. One of the main reasons I collect Lladró is its "extra mile" in detailing (e.g., the modeling in the jingle bell on the cat's collar). Sculptor: José Roig. $95–$125.

Francisco Catalá sculpted three miniature, rudimentarily modeled polar bears. Matte and glazed both retired in 1991. Here is "Teddy Bear" (#393 G/M); the other two had equally "cutesy" English-language names: "Cuddly Bear" (#392 G/M, *seated with four on floor*) and "Honey Bear" (#391 G/M, *up on hind legs*). $25–$35 ea.

"Two Pups" (#1046 G) was retired in 2000 at a very modest last retail of $80. Sculptor: Antonio Ramos. $125–$150.

Another of my NAO favorites is this exceptionally well-modeled grouping of a Siamese cat with attitude rubbing up against an astonished cocker. "Dog and Cat in Harmony" (#1048) was retired in 2001. Sculptor: Regino Torrijos. $125–$150.

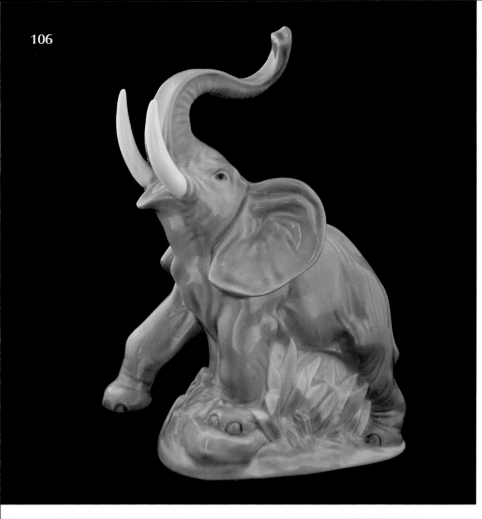

"Elephant" (model #106 G/M), matte retired 1991 and glazed in 2001. Was so pleased to find this one on the secondary market with no damage to tusks, trunk, and ears! Sculptor: Antonio Ruiz. $125–$150.

Below:
"Arctic Dreams" (NAO #1397 G) was issued in 2000 and retired in 2006 at a last retail price of $75. Sculptor: Begoña Jauregui. Courtesy of Joëlle Ley. $75–$100.

Like the two chicks also shown in this NAO gallery, "Foxy" (#366 G) was made with its body color right in the slip, eliminating the need to paint the entire surface the same basic color. The model was retired in 1984. Sculptor: José Roig. $125–$135.

CHAPTER 4

ZAPHIR

Zaphir was a relatively short-lived venture that began production sometime in the 1970s (ca. 1975, according to the official NAO website) and was phased out by 1982 or '83. (I base this dating on Zaphir models that appear in the 1983–84 NAO retail catalog. When Zaphir closed, its models then in production were taken over into the NAO brand; it is unlikely that this 1983–84 NAO catalogue could have been produced earlier than late 1983, so the appearance of former Zaphir models within it helps date the demise of the Zaphir brand.)

ARTE Y PORCELANAS, S.A. - Carretera de Torrente, 235 - Tel. 379 95 00 - 04 - 08 - CHIRIVELLA (Valencia)

Photo of the Zaphir factory from a 1978 retail catalog (note vintage of the car in foreground), located at Chirivella in the Valencia region. Although the brand name is prominently featured on the building's facade, there is nothing, either in building or catalog, to attest to an affiliation with Lladró.

Zaphir had a factory complex in Chirivella in the Valencia region of Spain. The earliest retail catalog I have for this brand was published in 1978, but it already featured a substantial corpus of models, many of which would later become NAO models when Zaphir was closed. Because of the depth of this catalog, I agree that 1975 is about right for Zaphir's start-up.

Along with the Zaphir catalog, I also have a 1981 Zaphir price list. There is nothing either in the catalog or the price list that directly affiliates the brand with Lladró. The signage on the factory building pictured in the catalog likewise doesn't reference Lladró. The only clue in the catalog to any Lladró connection at all is a photo captioned "Our sculptor Mr. José Puche Hernandez"—the same José Puche featured in photos of Lladró sculptors in company books and catalogs for the core Lladró collection.

In fact, as they did on the NAO line, several Lladró sculptors seem also to have worked on Zaphir. At least some of the sculptors for models that were eventually folded into the NAO brand are identified in NAO's own web catalog, and since the models in the two brands are identical (save for the colors), we can logically conclude that the identified sculptors for the NAO versions were the sculptors for the earlier Zaphir versions. The sculptor names that are most often associated with Zaphir models are Puche and José Roig, but Zaphir models were apparently also sculpted by Francisco Catalá, Vicente Martinez, Fulgencio García (not surprisingly!), and even (in at least two cases) Salvador Furió.

In cases where models were brought over into NAO, we can usually tell who the sculptor was from NAO records, but many Zaphir models were retired prior to the close of the brand. For those earlier Zaphir retirements, the sculptor is indicated as unknown in the photo captions of this book.

The mark for this brand was the brand name itself in an elaborate green script with a period after it (see the marks in appendix 1). The mark had no pictorial logo. The script in the mark made the name difficult to decipher, with the initial *Z* and the ending *n* giving the most trouble. I have seen the brand name rendered variously in online auctions and secondary-market price tags as Laphin, Laphir, and Zaphin.

A tip for collectors: whenever the name is misspelled in an online auction description or elsewhere on the secondary market, it means the seller doesn't know what he/she has. So a good bet for identifying reasonably priced Zaphir at online auctions is to type the most typical *misspellings* into the search field and see what comes up in the listings. I am not necessarily recommending online auctions, however, as an acquisition strategy for collectible porcelain. One of my most disappointing experiences purchasing Lladró products at internet auction involved a Zaphir with minor damage not considered significant enough to the seller to mention but significant enough to a collector that I wouldn't have bid had I known about it. However, Zaphir remains affordable, so I wasn't out a great deal of money and decided to keep the item despite the minor damage.

BRAND HISTORY

Not unlike its NAO predecessor, it is difficult to know how to account for the Zaphir brand or exactly where to place it in the broader context of Lladró company history. Was Zaphir yet one more renegade effort by Lladró sculptors to strike out on their own? Or was Zaphir a venture started under Lladró's own auspices—and, if so, why would Lladró have done that, given that it already had the NAO brand as one other well-established alternate brand? Why would the company dissipate its focus and resources—not to mention further confusing its consumers—with yet a third brand? The origins of this Zaphir brand are, to borrow a phrase from Winston Churchill, "a riddle wrapped in a mystery inside an enigma."

At one point, I thought Zaphir could have been the renegade company (more about which in chapter 6) that José Lladró describes in his memoir, *Passenger of Life*. According to José Lladró, the offending company was started by two defecting

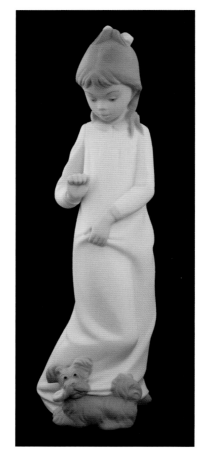

"My Playful Puppy" (Zaphir #595 M) was sculpted by José Roig, one of Lladró's core collection sculptors. It's one of the models brought over into the NAO brand when Zaphir was closed out, and retained the same model number in its NAO version. $75–$100.

"Boy with Candle" (Zaphir #567 G) later became a NAO. Sculptor: Julio Fernandez. Courtesy of Carlos D. Zepeda Abrego. $75–$100.

At left, Zaphir's "Girl Yawning" (#561 G/M, later made as NAO with the same serial number), not to be confused with "Boy Awakening" *at right*, made first as NAO #66 and later as the core Lladró brand #8870. (I know, it's head-spinning!) Sculptor for both models: Fulgencio García. $75–$100 ea.

collaborators of theirs and was put out of business by the Lladró brothers in a short but metaphorically bloody brand war that finally ended up in court, with Lladró prevailing. He writes that after the judge ruled in favor of the Lladró brothers, "We then agreed to talk to our ex-collaborators: *we bought part of their company* [my italics] and offered them a job again."[1] José Lladró then adds, with evident satisfaction, "That company turned out to be unimportant to us and closed down shortly afterwards. . . . The Chirivella was abandoned, sitting with its windows broken for many years."[2] Hmmm . . . two sculptors. The names of Puche and Roig do figure prominently in the Zaphir brand. Zaphir was located in Chirivella, and so was the renegade brand mentioned in Lladró's memoir, but then, so are a lot of other porcelain manufactories, including NAO!

Moreover, the chronology doesn't fit for Zaphir as the renegade company. Lladró writes that the conflict in question occurred in the 1960s, but I can find no evidence of Zaphir production prior to the mid-1970s. (See chapter 6 for my best guess, on the basis of model evidence, as to the actual identity of the renegade brand.) In any event and for whatever reason, Lladró (or Lladró sculptors) found themselves, for a few years in the late '70s and early '80s, with a third brand. When, for whatever other reason, Zaphir was closed in 1982–83, many of its models then still in production were brought over into the

NAO brand, which accounts for the identical models (though usually in a different color palette) found with NAO or Zaphir backstamps, or both. The NAO versions kept the same model numbers as had been assigned to them in Zaphir.

I discovered a further curiosity related to the Zaphir name in a 1981 price list for the NAO brand. Prominently displayed on the first page of the list is the name of the distributor: Zaphir (USA) Distribution Corp., the same corporate name found on the Zaphir price list for that same year. (Incidentally, as in the Zaphir price list, there is no mention of the Lladró name anywhere on the NAO price list, which is simply headed with the stylized letters of the old NAO logo and the subheading "NAO Collection.") This was a pattern in Lladró forays into brand diversification: shielding the Lladró name and reputation from possible failure of an alternate brand by deliberately omitting any reference to the parent company in the marketing literature. Given the retention of the Zaphir name as the "distribution company" in this price list, it's quite probable that, unlikely as adding yet another brand may seem as a winning strategy, Zaphir was a direct Lladró brand diversification effort by the Lladró company itself rather than a renegade offshoot.

In any case, Zaphir did not survive as a retail brand. Whatever Zaphir's initial origins, it was owned by Lladró by the time it ceased production sometime around 1982–83. Any models then in production that Lladró thought were salvageable were taken over into the NAO brand.

CHARACTERISTICS OF ZAPHIR

Zaphir themes are very similar to those in the regular Lladró brand and in NAO. Regular porcelain Zaphir was made both in glazed and matte forms. Just a few models were made in the Gres porcelain formula, most of them large birds or busts of animals.

Zaphir's human models are often quite large, at just under to well over a foot tall. There are certainly models in Lladró's core collection that are this large, but Zaphir seems to have made proportionately more models in that size range. This is just a few inches shy of the outer range of size for porcelain models because, as previously noted, porcelain, as a material, doesn't allow for large-scale models.

Model styles and detailing in Zaphir range from extremely simple to quite complex, and the aesthetic quality is variable. Generally speaking, one doesn't

A catalog photo of Zaphir's Flamenco dancers (#s 666 and 667 G) retailed in a 1981 price list at $85 ea. That price for these little misshapen characters might be difficult to sustain today. Sculptor unknown. Photos from a 1978 retail catalog.

Zaphir Enamel/Gres models include these animal/bird studies from a 1978 retail catalog photo. *Left to right*, tiger cub (Zaphir #107), goose pair (Zaphir #108), and "Alsatian" (Zaphir #103). "Alsatian" listed in 1981 at $72.50. Sculptor unknown; none of the Zaphir Gres models came over into NAO. Photos from a 1978 retail catalog. $250–$300 ea.

"Street Musicians" (Zaphir #684), later issued as NAO, same model number but slightly different colors. Zaphir's price in 1981 was already $420, a price level that seemed no deterrent to its NAO sales over the next two decades, where its last retail price in 1999 was $550! Sculptor: José Puche. Photos from a 1978 retail catalog.

Zaphir bust of a strong, regal "African Woman" (#111) is unique to that brand. Sculptor is unknown. It retailed at $340 back in 1981, and its value would be at least twice that today. Photos from a 1978 retail catalog.

Generalization, however, fails to do justice to the best of the Zaphir brand, which also has some incomparably fine models not found elsewhere in the Lladró corpus:

The colorful Gres model of crested "Cranes" (#105)

An unidentified model of a peasant woman with a cow (#580)

An untitled pair of bluebirds on the wing (#540, see p. 114)

"My Pet Sheep" (#628), a large and extraordinarily well-modeled grouping of a shepherd boy with his hand on a lamb standing next to him

An untitled girl swimming with dolphin (#639)

A Gres bust of a regal and dignified African woman (#111)

Zaphir's "It's Cold" (Zaphir model #520) was retired before the great transition to NAO. Collector Carlos Abrego has this model made in regular porcelain. Variant model here features enamel paint on the knit cap, external to the matte surface of the rest of the figurine. Sculptor unknown. $75–$125.

see the technical virtuosity or detailing in Zaphir that one sees in the other two brands. Many of the models of children are nondescript, and some are even grotesquely if deliberately misshapen (e.g., the series model #s 685–688 and the pair of child Flamenco dancers #s 666 and 667).

There is much less use of flowerwork in Zaphir than in the main Lladró brand. Yet, the retail price points for Zaphir models in 1981 were surprisingly high. (In fact, the Zaphir price structure appears to have been retained in the model transition to the NAO line, and this may be one of the pressures that pushed NAO prices beyond their originally intended price niche.)

In comparing the Zaphir price list from 1981 with a regular-collection Lladró price list from the very same year, the Lladró list shows a much-broader price range, with many very expensive pieces in the several hundreds and even thousands of dollars. Both lists offer prices at the lowest end of the range $100 and under—even $50 and under. The most expensive Zaphir on the 1981 price list is "Michael's Gang" at $820, and nothing else on its list even comes close to the higher-end ranges in the regular Lladró collection, so Zaphir is certainly not competing with Lladró at the upper end of the Lladró range. But at the range from $225 to $450, Zaphir offers a surprising number of items that would have been competing with Lladró's core brand at those price points.

Zaphir called its Gres models "Enamels," and the animal models, in particular, may be this brand's finest. From a 1978 retail catalog photo, "Eagle" (model #101, *at top*) and "Cranes" grouping (*bottom*, #105). Retail price on the eagle in 1981 was $235; on the cranes, $280. Sculptor unknown. Photos from a 1978 retail catalog. $350–$400 ea.

In addition to these singular Zaphir models not found elsewhere, the brand also contributed, when it was withdrawn from production, some of the best of its models to the NAO brand, where they proved immensely popular sellers:

"Michael's Gang" (#679)

"Street Musicians" (#684)

"Careless Maiden" (#642)

"Windswept" (#658), with its dynamic swirl of leaves, skirts, and hair answering the challenge of how to depict wind in porcelain

An unnamed model of a woman with Cupid (#649)

An unnamed model of a woman in elongated old-Lladró style, standing with a flat fishing basket under one arm, her other hand resting atop the head of a small boy holding a toy sailboat (#672, see p. 38)

ZAPHIR'S COLLECTING APPEAL

In the decade or less of its existence, the Zaphir brand thus produced not only a number of models that were never made in other Lladró brands, but also some (e.g., #s 649 and 672) that were produced in the NAO line for such a short time as to make them relatively scarce in either brand. Consequently, Zaphir, like NAO before it, offers expanded possibilities in Lladró collecting. And because it is considerably less well known among dealers than even NAO is, Zaphir models tend to be, for the most part, very affordable on the secondary market.

Two other advantages of Zaphir collecting are that it has escaped the unwelcome attentions of counterfeiters (good luck forging its scripted mark!), and there has been no mark tampering or marketing of seconds.

Collecting caveats are the same as those for NAO: be careful not to pay too much for Zaphir models, and don't buy them damaged. That said, though, if I could ever find any of the non-NAO models in the best of Zaphir listed above, I'd be willing to pay a bit extra just to have them!

Not much is known about Zaphir model #691G, a romantic grouping of a young medieval man and woman, one of the more complicated models produced in the Zaphir brand. Sculptor unknown. Photo from 1978 retail catalog. $200–$300.

A ZAPHIR SAMPLER

Above:
"Bluebirds" (#540 G), an original and unique Zaphir showing Lladró sculptors' unparalleled ability to create aerodynamic models. The technical risks this involves are one of the characteristics that separates Lladró products from imitators. Sculptor unknown. Courtesy of Carlos D. Zepeda Abrego. $150–$175.

Hard to imagine how many molds it would have taken to make "Michael's Gang" (Zaphir/NAO #679), later to become NAO's "Boys Playing Cards." Its last retail price in the NAO brand in 2000 was $1,130! Sculptor: José Puche. Photo from 1978 Zaphir retail catalog.

An iconic figure in Spanish culture, thus also in Lladró brands, "Don Quixote" (Zaphir #636 G/M) moved to NAO, retaining the same model number, when Zaphir closed. Last retail on glazed NAO version in 2001 was $630. Sculptor: unspecified but probably Salvador Furió. Photo from 1978 Zaphir retail catalog.

Zaphir's "Poodle" (#518 G) was made only in that brand. Modeling is more rudimentary and facial expression more whimsical than the Lladró core collection "Poodle" (see chapter 1). Sculptor unknown. $100–$125.

Don Quixote's chubby sidekick and manservant, Sancho Panza, also appears in all Lladró brands. In this Zaphir version, Sancho holds Don Quixote's shield. Model number and sculptor unknown. Courtesy of Carlos D. Zepeda Abrego. $100–$125.

Long-haired dachshund; Zaphir mark, model number, and sculptor unknown. Courtesy of Carlos D. Zepeda Abrego. $100–$125.

Above:
"Guess Who?" (Zaphir #655 G) is classic! (Can't you just hear the open-mouthed boy yelling, "Ach! You're chokin' me!") I believe this was a unique Zaphir model, probably retired before the brand was closed. Sculptor unknown. Courtesy of Carlos D. Zepeda Abrego. $150–$175.

Left:
"Girl with Rabbit" (Zaphir/NAO #522 G/M) was moved to the NAO brand when Zaphir closed. Sculptor unknown. $75–$100.

Below:
"It's Raining" (Zaphir #656 G/M) appears to have been another unique model in Zaphir; I find no evidence that it ever became a NAO. The umbrella pole is metal, and the handle is porcelain, as is the rest of the model. Sculptor unknown. $125–$150.

Left:
"Potato Farmer" (model #570 G) had a last Zaphir price of $85. It experienced a new life as a NAO but was retired after just a year or two at a last NAO retail price of $72. Sculptor unknown. Courtesy of Carlos D. Zepeda Abrego. $75–$100.

Above right:
Zaphir's "Ostrich" (#716 G), one of my favorite Zaphirs ever since I saw it in this photo! (Check out that facial expression and those big feet poking out from under the feathers.) Model is unique to Zaphir. Courtesy of Carlos D. Zepeda Abrego. $125–$150.

Left:
Unidentified Zaphir clown model has a vaguely creepy face painting that makes me see why some people find clowns scary! Model number and sculptor unknown. Courtesy of Carlos D. Zepeda Abrego. $75–$100.

CHAPTER 5

GOLDEN MEMORIES

The ill-fated and somewhat ironically named "Golden Memories" brand was in production for only three years, from 1991 to 1993. Golden Memories (GM) had a large production inventory, with much of it still circulating on the secondary market. It happens also to be the only Lladró brand in which one can clearly see a direct and intentional brand diversification strategy at work.[1]

At first, GM wasn't conceived of as a separate brand at all but, rather, as a kind of "special collection" within the NAO brand (which is how they're identified in a 1991 NAO price list, using the serial numbering for the NAO brand). Soon thereafter, someone at the parent company got the none-too-felicitous idea of spinning GM off as a distinct brand, targeted to the lower end of the porcelain figurine market that was already dominated by Enesco's Precious Moments®. The three years of GM production resulted in three distinct styles as Lladró cast about to get it right in a lower-end market segment with which it was profoundly unfamiliar.

Part of the trouble was that, as with Lladró's other less intentional brand diversification forays, in order to avoid compromising the Lladró name if the venture didn't work out, the GM mark did not identify the brand as Lladró. The trade-off for shielding the Lladró name was that the new GM brand didn't get to benefit from association with its famous parent company. At the same time, the popularity of Precious Moments® in that price niche was buoyed by that brand's own distinctive and immediately recognizable style and aesthetic.

Price point was perhaps Lladró's biggest vulnerability in trying to break into the lower end of the porcelain figurine market. Most Golden Memories figurines retailed in the $60–$100 range, and several retailed for over $100, at which point they were in price competition with the manufacturer's own NAO brand. Except for small ornaments, Lladró couldn't seem to bring GM prices under that range and still cover the costs of production. Most Precious Moments® models, by contrast, could be purchased in the $25–$40 retail range, significantly lower than even the low-end range for Golden Memories.

"Friend in Tow" (#33010), a first-year GM, when models looked most like Lladró though nothing in the mark identified them as such. This model would later become NAO's "Traveling Girl" (NAO #1038 G), recently retired at $85. Sculptor: Antonio Ramos.

"Clown Magic" (GM #3309), another of the first-year models. Despite the popularity of clown models, the retail price of $120 was too rich for the market GM was targeting. Later became NAO's "Now You See It" (NAO #485), retired in 2001 at a last retail of $185. Sculptor: Regino Torrijos.

First-year "Injured Pup" (GM #33015) would later become NAO's "A Friend in Need" (NAO #1050), retired in 2001 at $80. Sculptor: Antonio Ramos.

CHARACTERISTICS OF THE BRAND

The defining characteristic of the Golden Memories brand in relation to other Lladró brands was that, throughout its three-year history, its models were devoted exclusively to children and childhood themes—not entirely coincidentally, the focus of Enesco's Precious Moments® as well. The mark adopted for the GM brand was a green backstamp whose logo consisted of the silhouette of a child lying on his stomach amid grass and flowers and facing a small dog.

The most aesthetically successful GM models were those from the first year, whose modeling had the most affinity with child models in other Lladró. First-year models of Golden Memories were done in a unique unglazed porcelain that was translucent when held up to light. The tactile feel of a first-year GM is also quite deliciously silky. The color palette is distinctly un-Lladró-like, with vivid pastel colors over a bright ivory ground. These two unusual aspects of the models—their distinctive finish and color palette—combined with the lack of Lladró affiliation in their mark meant that the models really had to compete on their own merits with the modestly priced but volume-lucrative market that was already owned by the Precious Moments® brand. By the end of the first year, it had become obvious that Lladró's strategy for penetrating that market was in trouble.

For the second year of GM's short life, Lladró retired all the first-year Golden Memories models and did a major appearance overhaul for the brand. The faces on the GM children now had large, dark eyes, and the noses and faces were inexplicably flattened. I've always thought of these second-year models as being the proverbial "faces only a mother could love." None of them smile, and they all look vaguely miserable. As a means of differentiating the brand in the market, they were certainly *different*, but it's hard to imagine, in hindsight, how this particular difference could possibly have translated into retail success. (Large eyes, serious and distinctive faces . . . I can imagine a GM marketing team sitting around wracking its collective brain for what made Precious Moments® so distinctive and coming up with these second-year figurines in an attempt to riff on Precious Moments® without actually copying an aesthetic that they didn't understand anyway.)

Thus it came to pass that in its third and last year, GM got its final facelift. Models were made in thin, glazed porcelain that, as in the first-year figures, was translucent when held up to light, in contrast to the more opaque porcelain of the second year. Eyes on faces were large, round, and uncharacteristically dark for Lladró, not unlike the eyes in the second-year figures. The faces, however, became more pleasingly rounded, the noses and cheeks more defined and less "smooshed" than those of the brand's second year, and, while the kids still aren't smiling openly, they do look a whole lot happier! The phrase "from the Lladró family of products" was finally added to the mark, but the basic aesthetic was still so far afield of anything else Lladró that the identification was superfluous: people simply didn't recognize GM figurines as Lladró, and casual shoppers wouldn't necessarily have picked them up to look at the mark on the base.

Speaking of bases, the shape of the base became an odd marketing gimmick for third-year models, indicating thematic subcategories within the overall collection: crescent moon (for "magical evenings"), star (for "heavenly themes and the world of entertainment"), heart (for "romantic themes"), and cloverleaf (for "themes evoking nature and the imaginary world of tiny forest dwellers" [e.g., elves and fairies]).[2] These categories were more or less arbitrarily populated (e.g., a model of a little Japanese girl in kimono stands on a heart-shaped base, while a companion piece is kneeling on a clover leaf, neither model being consistent with their base categories as described in the catalog).

This photo of "Southern Belle" (#33107) from a 1993–94 GM catalog shows the flattened face and pug nose characteristic of second-year GM figures, making them all look as if they depicted the unfortunate members of the same unattractive family. Small wonder the third-year figures demanded a complete facelift!

"Pretty Like Mom" (#34002) and "Guess Who, Dad?" (#34001) from GM's third year. Cute, but so far afield of other Lladró that even the belated mark addition, "From the Lladró Family of Products," couldn't save them—certainly not while retailing at more than $100 apiece. Photo from 1993–94 GM retail catalog.

Left to right, third-year GM "Oriental Grace"(#34028) and "Oriental Celebration" (#34036). GM models were children, lending their costume a kind of "dress-up" character. Here, the heart- and clover-shaped bases have nothing obvious to do with the catalog-stated themes for those symbols. Photo from 1993–94 GM retail catalog.

Among the oddest of Golden Memories creations were several third-year figural lamps in the form of houses: "Gingerbread House" (#34023), "Teacup Tales" (#34024, whose base form was an inverted teacup), and "Teapot Tales" (#34017, whose base form was a teapot). Though they may have had merit as an appeal to childhood fantasy, they functioned more as atmospheric night lights than actual lamps and were expensive given their limited use—$225 retail for the gingerbread house and $175 for the teapot house (the teacup house was "only" $135).

The GM brand was mercifully discontinued in 1994. Most of the first-year models went into the NAO line (ironically, the starting point for the original GM concept). As NAO models, they acquired the glazed finish and porcelain colors more typical of that brand, where they did rather well and where several of them are still in production today. None of the second- or third-year GM models survived the brand's demise. The success of the first-year GM models after their transfer to the NAO brand underscores that the problem with them was not in the models themselves, but in the marketing rationale and niche strategy Lladró had developed for the GM brand and the company's lack of experience with or understanding of the lower tier of the porcelain collectibles market.

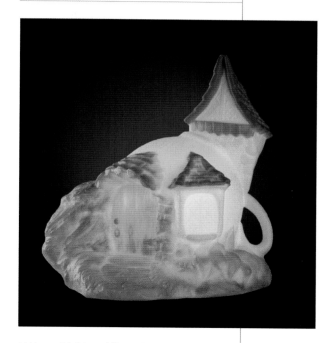

Making models lit from within must have seemed a natural, given GM's translucent porcelain, but "Teacup Tales" (#34024, *left*) and "Teapot Tales" (#34017, *right*) would have been more night lights than lamps dispersing light into a room. Combined retail price topped $300 USD. Photos from a 1993–94 GM retail catalog.

COLLECTING CONSIDERATIONS

I find the first-year Golden Memories charming and have a few in my own collection, acquired at very low prices on the secondary market. As was the case with my NAO "Goose," I bought my first pair of GM figures when I was fairly new to Lladró collecting and because I was absolutely sure they were Lladró products despite the lack of attribution in the mark.

Although I have seen them on the secondary market, I have none of the flat-faced second-year GM models in my collection, and no plans to acquire any. I have only one third-year figure: "Trick or Treat" (GM model #34006), a child with a freckled face, dressed in a spooky, white-hooded Halloween costume and standing on a crescent moon base with a jack-o'-lantern at his feet. I was charmed by the theme and by the light sprinkling of freckles across the child's nose—the kind of careful detailing that I associate with Lladró.

Generally speaking, the most valuable of the Golden Memories models are those from that first year (i.e., those that have the most affinity with a recognizably Lladró style). However, bearing in mind that many of those models can also be found in the NAO brand, I'm afraid the conclusion is pretty much inescapable that, with few exceptions, GM models do not hold their retail value. If I really want a particular example that I find on the secondary market, I usually won't pay more than $45 as an upper limit.

Like Tang and Rosal (see chapter 6), Golden Memories is more of a collecting curiosity than a collecting enthusiasm in its own right. Lladró collectors may want at least a GM example or two for their own collections, but I'd advise against collecting large quantities of it. The usual advice to avoid the purchase of damaged pieces goes double for GM, since they will never be worth the cost of restoring them.

In a nutshell, the main problem the Golden Memories brand presented for Lladró was that the company couldn't make them cheaply enough to appeal to consumers in the down-market niche for which they were intended. This retail problem has affected secondary-market values as well, and in lieu of assigning the same price range to every picture caption in the GM gallery that follows, I would simply say at the outset that, in most cases, the value of any one GM model would be in the $45–$50 range. At any price above that, shoppers could well find something on the secondary market in one of the other Lladró brands.

Irresistible "Trick or Treat" ghost (#34006), the only third-year GM model I have. Freckles on cheeks, not visible in the photo, are characteristic of Lladró's dedication to detail even in GM, its least expensive brand. Crescent moon base is consistent with marketing literature reserving that shape for "magical evenings."

Yes, for many collectors, even dealer/advertising plaques are a thing! Here's the porcelain dealer plaque for "Golden Memories," with the Lladró attribution tagline that was added to the mark in the second year. Courtesy of Carlos D. Zepeda Abrego.

Opposite page
Top: "None for You!" (#33013) would later be made as NAO #1045, with a different thematic interpretation in the title: "Puppy's Birthday." The NAO version is still in production at a retail cost of $85, but the GM version on the secondary market should cost considerably less.

Bottom: These are, I believe, the only animal models made in the otherwise entirely child-centered GM brand, each in a "gift box": *clockwise from left*, "Box of Mischief" (#33050), "Poodles in a Box" (#33052), and "Playful Bunnies" (#33051). Each of these would later reprise as NAO.

A
GOLDEN
MEMORIES
SAMPLER

Left to right, "Come Home Soon" (#33012) and "Lullaby" (#33030). These were my very first GM models, found in an antique store, and, once again, I knew instinctively they were Lladró despite the unusual coloring and the lack of attribution in the first-year mark. These would later become, respectively, NAO's "Boy on Phone with Puppets" (#1044) and "Sleepyhead with Lamby" (#1029).

Above:
The yellow ducky on the baby's bib on "Plenty to Eat" (#33407) is an especially endearing touch. The model would later become "Souptime" (NAO #1075 G, with a blue ducky), now also retired at a last retail price of $55 in 1997.

Left:
Aptly named "Frisky Friend" (#33003), this first-year GM was later made as NAO #1054 G with the nondescript title "Girl Followed by Puppy."

"On My Way" (GM #33040) needs a 360-degree view to appreciate all its elements, from bow tie and facial decoration on the front to the umbrella and old kit bag at back. It would later become NAO's "Travelin' Man" (NAO #486), retired in 1998 at a hefty last retail price of $185!

OTHER LLADRÓ AND LLADRÓ-AFFILIATED BRANDS (ROSAL, TANG, HISPANIA)

Several other relatively little-known brands of Spanish porcelain have a more or less direct affiliation with Lladró. They are difficult to find on the secondary market and, in two cases, are not only difficult to identify but also sometimes impossible to authenticate with certainty because they are not cataloged and are usually found unmarked, for reasons explained in this chapter.

ROSAL AND THE WAR OF THE BRANDS

Rosal was a brand invented by the Lladró brothers expressly and solely for the purpose of putting a competing brand out of business. José Lladró tells the tale in a chapter of his memoir titled "A Providential Conflict."[1] Apparently, two Lladró sculptors and a chemist defected from the Lladró company in the early to mid-1960s and set up their own competing company, which José Lladró doesn't name. (I can imagine this as being the source of the stubbornly persistent false rumor, heard right up to the present day, that one of the Lladró brothers had broken off from the other two to start his own company.) Although his memoir doesn't name the sculptors, either, we might deduce, on the basis of a comment made just a few pages earlier in the memoir, that one of them was the famous early Lladró sculptor Fulgencio García; Lladró describes García as "a restless man who gave us many headaches, as will be seen further on."[2] In an apparent editing glitch, this tantalizing reference remains frustratingly unfulfilled in the remaining pages of his book; Lladró never again mentions García's name. However, just a few pages after that initial reference, José writes about the "Providential Conflict," so it is reasonable to conclude that García was involved in that conflict, perhaps even the ringleader of it.

It's clear from José Lladró's description that the brothers regarded this defection as a personal betrayal by some of their earliest collaborators. The Lladrós were not only profoundly hurt and profoundly angered but also profoundly determined to make their former collaborators pay for what was perceived as their treachery.

This pair of Spaniels has a blue "Made in Spain" mark but is otherwise unattributed. Such fine work could come only from a Lladró sculptor and is likely a Tang or Rosal from which the original paper label had gone missing. Courtesy of Brad Welch.

The brothers' keen sense of injury over this defection is at least a bit surprising if we consider that the behavior of their collaborators essentially amounted to the same thing the brothers themselves had done when they fell out with their first two employers and struck out on their own rather than subjugate their own artistic interests as hirelings of others. The importance of the brothers' early "branching out" has been celebrated in company books and marketing literature and must surely have been mentioned in celebratory fashion at least a time or two in the hearing of employees.

Be that as it may, the renegades' tactics apparently involved, to use José Lladró's term, "flooding" local markets with the competing brand (though one wonders what that verb could have meant in any literal sense for a small start-up competitor in the 1960s), offered at a price to undercut Lladró in these markets. Because the style was naturally similar to Lladró, since the owners of the new brand were themselves Lladró sculptors, the tactic worked. While José Lladró's memoir makes it clear he considered the products of the competing brand inferior to Lladró, the upstart product was good enough that, as the memoir also makes plain, the Lladrós considered it a genuine threat not only to Lladró's market share but to its very existence as a company.

The Lladrós decided to fight fire with fire. They developed a brand they called "Rosal" ("to prevent the Lladró name from being jeopardized"[3]) whose sole purpose was to go head to head with the insurgent brand and put it out of business.

The name "Rosal" was probably constructed from Rosa and the initial *L* (as in Rosa Lladró). Eldest brother Juan Lladró's daughter is named Rosa, but, more to the point, so was the Lladrós' mother, that towering figure in their development whose ambition for her sons' advancement stopped at nothing. It seems an auspicious name for a brand meant to pull out all the stops to make sure the Lladrós were the ones left standing when the dust cleared.

Rosal's simpler style relative to other Lladró made it easier and less expensive to produce, thereby allowing Lladró to respond effectively and with speed to the price point advantage enjoyed by the renegades. Apparently, the Lladró strategy was, in its turn, successful in undermining the efforts of the competing brand.

If the brothers had been blindsided by the renegade entrepreneurs' competing venture, they were gobsmacked by the rebels' next move: suing the Lladró brothers for copyright infringement. It was a bold strategy that hauled the Lladrós into court, in the person of José Lladró as company representative. José acquitted himself and his brothers well enough to win the case. In what he presents in his book as a gesture of magnanimity, the Lladrós agreed to give their former collaborators their old jobs back. Actually, the Lladrós may not have had a choice; a characteristic of Spanish employment law at the time was that an acquiring company couldn't just fire or lay off employees from the acquired company, as it might be allowed to do under the American legal principle of "employment at will." Under the Spanish legal principle of "stability of employment," a company in Spain incurred the employer obligations of the original owner toward an acquired company's employees. This could well account for much of Lladró's brand diversification, since the company would not have been allowed just to quit acquired brands without hiring the employees who came with them, but whom Lladró may not have been in a position to absorb into its core manufactory. (Recent changes in Spanish employment law are more favorable to employers and make layoffs and terminations at least somewhat easier.)

Having bought what was presumably a controlling interest in the competing company, the Lladró brothers were then in a position to do what they had wanted to do from the beginning: shut it down. Rosal did not remain in production, either, its sole retail purpose having now been fulfilled.

Because it was intended as a temporary marketing weapon, Lladró had spent no time developing a brand mark for Rosal. Consequently, identifying Rosal is a challenge for collectors; its retail identity was most often defined by a simple name sticker that could be removed shortly after purchase. Rarely, one does find a Rosal with a brand name impressed into the actual porcelain. Most Rosal was, however, permanently marked only with the country of origin, either impressed into the porcelain underbase or in a cobalt-blue backstamp. This legend, "Made in Spain," will be the only surviving mark on a formerly stickered item from which the paper has gone missing.

"Girl with Butterfly" is also marked "Made in Spain" with no brand attribution, but there's no mistaking a Lladró face. Most likely a Tang or Rosal.

IDENTICAL TWINS?
HOW ABOUT IDENTICAL TRIPLETS!

There is evidence that Lladró dipped back into some of its oldest models for its brand war ammunition. Bearing in mind, now, that this is the 1960s, and Lladró wouldn't have had that much of a corpus yet to dip back into for getting Rosal quickly to market (plus it was two sculptors down in its production staff as a result of the defections), Lladró reprised at least some of its decimal-numbered models as Rosal. Assuming Fulgencio García was a principal involved in the

Opposite page:
This romantic couple has all the characteristics of a very early Lladró but is also without a brand mark. The raised/enameled decoration on the woman's bodice is especially eye catching. Courtesy of Brad Welch.

This romantic couple has all the characteristics of a very early Lladró but is also without a brand mark. The raised/enameled decoration on the woman's bodice is especially eye catching. Courtesy of Brad Welch.

renegade brand, this, of course, would have been a proverbial slap in the face, since García was also the sculptor of record for most of the decimal-numbered Lladró models. (This could have been the basis for the renegades' charge of copyright infringement, since it is unknown who actually retained the design rights to these earliest models developed by García, and the fact that the suit was not upheld may indicate there was no documented evidence on that point.)

Specifically, the following items have been found with impressed Rosal marks: Lladró model #331.13 ("Pheasant") and #328.13 ("Polar Bear"), with a companion polar bear that was uncataloged in the regular brand. In fact, examples of these particular models have been found with one of *three* impressed marks: Lladró, NAO, and Rosal. The sculptor for the bears was Fulgencio García, but for the pheasant, Vicente Martinez. And is that merely coincidental, or have we just located the second renegade sculptor mentioned so cryptically in José Lladró's memoir—and is this yet another example of fighting the renegades with their own ammunition—that is, with the earliest Lladró models the straying sculptors themselves had designed? It's a tantalizing question, and while there's no way to know for certain on the basis of the available evidence, it would at least be a plausible explanation for some of the model choices Lladró made for the Rosal brand.

TANG: THE PROBABLE RENEGADE

At one point, I thought the renegade brand could have been NAO itself, but José Lladró's book clearly says that the brand in question was discontinued once Lladró acquired a controlling interest in it, and if that is correct, the renegade brand could not have been NAO, the only alternative Lladró brand still in business to this day. The renegade brand couldn't have been Zaphir, either, because that brand wasn't even around until more than a decade after the conflict in question.

In his memoir, José Lladró doesn't name either the competing brand or those who developed it; he seems to have felt it was just desserts for their names to be consigned to history's dustbin, at least as relates to this particular entrepreneurial venture. But by process of elimination and with respect to consistency in brand chronology and the fact that its models have a close affinity with other Lladró models, I have come to believe that the upstart was a brand called Tang.

Most of the few examples of Tang items I have seen show such exceptionally strong affinities with the Lladró style. Bear in mind that this is still the early to mid-1960s, too early in the Lladró company's life and reputation for non-Lladró companies to have attempted to jump on its bandwagon. However, while these affinities amounted to strong resemblance to the Lladró style, I had not, as of the publication of the first edition of this book, seen a Tang model that was an identical clone either of a known Lladró or a NAO model.

Then, in April 2016, I received an email from someone who had two Tang-marked models her parents had purchased many years ago on a trip to Spain. She sent me photos both of the models and the marks. One of these figurines was an identical twin to NAO's "Man's Best Friend (NAO #32), the sculptor for which was none other than Fulgencio García. It was the first example of a Tang item I could conclude was a Lladró model per se.

I have also seen an example of the NAO miniature "Seated Angel" (#11 G/M and, with that very low serial number, itself a very early issue) with a Tang mark. The Tang is modeled as an earthling without the wings, but in all other respects, the two models are identical.

A rare instance of a Tang model actually marked as such, with the mark impressed into the porcelain. (See the sticker photo shown in this chapter for a clearer view of this logo than a camera can capture from this impressed mark.)

Borzoi dog grouping, 14 inches long (unmarked Tang or Rosal with cobalt-blue "Made in Spain"). Only Lladró would take that risk of soaring legs and tails or pay such attention to detail in the dogs' heads—right down to the tongues and teeth! $250–$300.

Foil Tang sticker that was the only maker attribution on most items produced in this brand. Two of the more permanent marks on later items were impressed right into the porcelain base or as a cobalt-blue backstamp; both had the same form as the foil label.

This very strong circumstantial model evidence is sufficient to convince me that Tang was, in fact, the renegade brand referred to in Lladró's memoir, and that it, and the subsequent legal problems it caused for the Lladró brothers, accounts for José Lladró's cryptic reference some pages earlier in his memoir to the problems Fulgencio García posed for the Lladró brand. How one views this copyright dispute would depend in large part on the underlying question of who actually owned the models, a question we can't answer given the paucity of evidence for the contractual relationships between the Lladrós and the earliest sculptors who worked for them. Although the court sided with Lladró in the copyright suit, García may initially have felt free to re-create—in a new, independent brand—Lladró-brand models he may have himself created.

The Tang mark consisted only of the name in a kind of Asian-style lettering. It's unclear why the original owners of this brand would have chosen an Asian-sounding name—unless they were hoping to benefit from a halo association with the Tang dynasty of China, which is considered by many to be the golden age of Chinese art and culture. The Tang dynasty is perhaps most famous for its pottery tomb figures. The choice of this name for a line of porcelain figurines may have been intentional in order to benefit from these associations with a high point in the arts history of China as porcelain's birthplace.

Back to Spain, the Tang mark was sometimes impressed and at least sometimes consisted of a cobalt-blue backstamp. More often, it was identified only with a sticker such as that shown here, so that, as with Rosal, the only remaining indelible mark on the base (again, either impressed or in cobalt blue) is "Made in Spain." Thus, high-quality models with strong aesthetic affinities with Lladró and "Made in Spain" marks but no company attribution are most likely either Tang or Rosal from which the stickers have fallen off. Unfortunately, it is impossible to say which of the two brands such models are once the name stickers have gone missing, since neither brand survived long enough to produce a catalog.

Whatever the challenges for collectors in identifying specific models within the two brands, Tang and Rosal represent a fascinating chapter in the early evolution of the Lladró company. They also reveal that this evolution was quite a bit rockier than glossy company marketing literature might lead us to believe, even if common sense and personal experience might already have clued us in that such an amazing venture as Lladró doesn't happen without a few bumps in the road.

A Hispania leopard cub, one of the life-sized animal models made in a nonporcelain ceramic body after Lladró acquisition of the Hispania company. Primary colors and aesthetic style bear little relation to anything else Lladró made; the Lladró attribution is confirmed by the DAISA copyright acronym in the mark.

THE HISPANIA BRAND

When the Lladró brothers opened their first store in the 1950s, they often bought materials for resale from Hispania, which José Lladró described in his memoir as "an innovative and imaginative Manises company that created quality products that were modern for that time."[4] Having long admired its products, the brothers found themselves in a position to buy the Hispania company in the 1980s. Hispania made mostly decorative and nonfigural domestic items in a ceramic, nonporcelain body.

The brothers continued this tradition, adding to it, however, several animal models that are of special interest. The unusual characteristics of these "Hispania by Lladró" animal models included their nearly life-size forms and their primary, naturalistic colors. It's apparent that relatively few of them would have been made in the few short years Lladró owned the Hispania brand before closing it, and they remain of keen interest to Lladró collectors aware of them. The combination of secondary-market demand and relative scarcity, plus the inherent appeal and cross-collectibility of animal models generally and especially ones this large, has served to drive prices up for the Hispania animal models, even at internet auctions, where I've seen them go as high as $200. (It should be mentioned here that other Hispania items, consisting mostly of decorative, nonfigural house wares, have only nominal value [$25 or less], even those produced during Lladró's ownership.)

An additional factor contributing to the scarcity of Hispania animal models is their fragility. They are made of nonporcelain ceramic and are surprisingly light and thin walled given their size, which, unfortunately, makes them vulnerable to damage. However, porcelain, a more durable if expensive substance, does not lend itself to the production of very large models, as European porcelain inventor Meissen discovered early in its history when it attempted to make large porcelain figurines. Consequently, the only way for Lladró to produce nearly life-size animals would have been in Hispania's nonporcelain ceramic.

Hispania items dating from Lladró's ownership do not include the Lladró name and are—typically for Lladró's forays into other brands—identified only by the addition of the "DAISA" copyright notice to the logo and mark. Items without this copyright notice predate Lladró's ownership of the brand.

A girl with poncho in a matte finish isn't marked at all, not even with an attribution to the country of origin. But once again, there's just no mistaking a Lladró face.

It's also important to note, in avoiding collector confusion, that when Lladró dropped this brand, it seems also to have dropped any rights it may have had to the name. Subsequently, the Nadal company (not affiliated with Lladró, and about which, more later in this chapter) picked up the name for a collection of figurines within its broader brand.

COLLECTING CONSIDERATIONS AND CAVEATS

With each of the brands mentioned in this chapter, some collector cautions are in order. Contrary to popular belief, rarity does not automatically equate to higher value. Rarity can be canceled out by a lack of shared knowledge of particular brands or models among potential collectors, and a consequent lack of independent demand for the models and brands in question (demand being the primary generator for value). For example, many rare items in the Lladró main brand are well known to collectors, even if only by photograph, so there has always been a strong interest in and desire to own them.

Rosal and Tang, on the other hand, were never cataloged for collector purposes; consequently, collectors don't know the models in these brands beyond the occasional example that may surface on the secondary market. The fact that many of both these brands had only the country of origin as part of their indelible marks, with the brand name being identified solely by a removable sticker usually no longer present, further complicates efforts to authenticate them. These ambiguities tend to cancel out rarity as a consideration for the value of items made in these brands. This is not to say that either brand doesn't remain desirable for veteran collectors with a particular interest in the historical evolution of the Lladró company; it is merely to point out that it is difficult to place a particular value on any given example of a Tang or Rosal. For these models, especially, the answer to the question "What is it worth?" is "Whatever another collector would pay you for it." The specifics of that answer will have to be decided in the marketplace in individual transactions between buyers and sellers.

There are two exceptions to that rule for these lesser-known brands. One is animal models. Even in instances where a model does not quite rise to the standard in the core collection, the quality of the modeling in Rosal and Tang animal models will still serve their future value well in comparison to the many unmarked, dime-store knickknacks flooding the secondary market. In part because of the cross-collectible appeal of animal models and because of their unusual size, the nearly life-size animals made in Hispania by Lladró can also stand on their own merits, even independent of their association with Lladró.

Not to gild the lily, I've chosen for comparison a Lladró competitor's "best in show." Model is tucked in on itself, with hands molded to the body rather than separately articulated. Elements don't fit well together (formal wear, book, garden urn). Facial modeling is good, but eye painting is dark and heavy.

The other exception to nominal value is the decimal-numbered regular collection rarities that were produced in the Rosal brand. So few of these would have been made in any of the three brands where they have been found (Lladró, NAO, and Rosal) that any of these "identical triplets" would be able to command a price premium—the only remaining question being how much. Given that all were made by the same respected umbrella company and are rare in any Lladró brand, it's likely that discovery of clones of regular collection Lladró versions once considered impossibly rare will both elevate the value of the clones and bring the value of the regular-collection rarities down closer to the value of the clones—a sort of meeting in the middle between two extremes of an outmoded price continuum.

NAO's "Jolly Jester" (#1067 G, a.k.a. "Joy"), part of a series of three little charmers that included "Jangles" (#1065 G) and
"Jingles" (#1066 G). Sculptor for the series: José Puche. Retired in 2004 at a last retail price of $65 each.

"Charlie the Tramp" (a.k.a. "The Eternal Poet," Lladró #5233 G). Lladró ran afoul of Chaplin's estate over failure to obtain a license to use the image. The Chaplin estate's demand? Pay up or desist. Lladró chose to desist, retiring the model in 1991. Sculptor: Juan Huerta. $700–$750.

Mark you'll find on the base of Nadal porcelain figurines. Nadal is arguably the only current Spanish porcelain that can compete with Lladró for modeling quality. But you'd have trouble identifying retired models, since the company has no consumer catalogs and only keeps current models on its website.

A WORD ABOUT NON-LLADRÓ BRANDS

There are many small companies in Spain, particularly in the Valencia region, that are working "in the Lladró style" in preference to developing a style of their own. Most of these companies are, frankly, trying to cash in on Lladró's success and are hoping to capture some of the Lladró market by using the carrot of lower price—without, however, possessing an ability to produce Lladró's high quality. These brands can afford to undercut Lladró in price because the artisans who make them are far less skilled than Lladró artisans, don't take the technical risks that Lladró takes, and use far fewer molds to make what they make.

Generally speaking and with only one or two exceptions, these companies have no websites. None of them at all have retail or collector catalogs to help collectors identify individual models. They have little or no export presence beyond Spain and arrive in other countries largely via tourists' suitcases, whence they eventually end up on the secondary market when their original owners tire of them. Such items produce no end of consumer questions, confusion, and, ultimately, frustration; it's simply no fun to collect items that can't be specifically identified. Given all these limitations, the per-item value of non-Lladró models is nominal ($25 or less). I would advise people interested in collecting twentieth-century Spanish porcelain figurines to avoid these non-Lladró brands—with perhaps one exception, which I will come to shortly. There just doesn't seem to be any logical reason to spend $50 or more on an aesthetically inferior product when, for the same price on the secondary market, a lucky buyer can still find an occasional Lladró in one or another of its genuine brands.

The one possible exception to this general rule is Nadal Porcelains (a name not to be confused with the Nalda Brand mentioned in chapter 1 nor with a former US-based retail business of the name Nadal that sold Lladró products). Nadal is actually a much-older Spanish company than Lladró, having been founded more than 100 years ago, in 1915. This is the only company I know of that can approach Lladró in the quality of its models. Nadal's thematic interests are not as broad as those of Lladró, and its approach to those models is not as adventurous, but what Nadal does in the best of its models it does very well. A characteristic feature of recent Nadal porcelains is a combination of matte and shiny enamel surfaces in the same model, similar to Lladró's Gres but without the darker, earthy tones of Gres.

Unfortunately, consumers not living in Spain may find some of the same frustrations with Nadal that they would encounter in collecting other non-Lladró Spanish porcelain brands: no historical collector catalogs, little or no manufacturer support for secondary-market collecting, and no way to identify retired models. As of this writing, Nadal does have a website (in English and Spanish, www.nadalporcelana.com), where readers can browse current issues, but there is no historical catalog on that site. It should also be noted that with Lladró having abandoned the brand "Hispania," Nadal has picked up the name for one of its collections, the style of which bears no relation to what Lladró produced when it owned the name. Nadal also produces a collection called "Gaudí," which somewhat resembles a collection by the same name in Lladró, albeit less sophisticated in theme and execution and offered at much-lower retail price points than Lladró's Gaudí.

If you're looking for a lovely decorative accent for your home, Nadal is a fine choice. But if you're going to be frustrated by not knowing the identity of older models, when they were made, and how much they're worth, you'd be better served sticking with Lladró's two main brands, one named Lladró and the other named NAO.

CHAPTER 7

NEW DIRECTIONS FOR LLADRÓ AND LLADRÓ COLLECTORS

Although this is a book about retired models in Lladró brands, it seems important to say something about the recent evolution of the Lladró company and its future direction, particularly given major changes in the company that have had a direct impact on its porcelain division and, therefore, have potential impact on the Lladró secondary market.

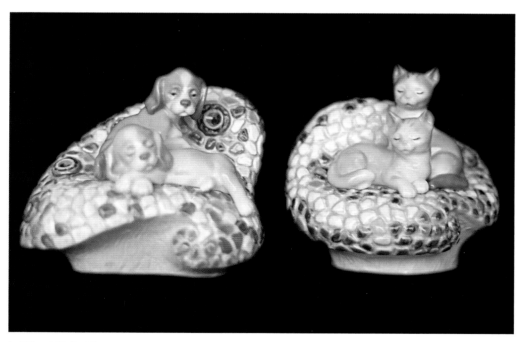

In 1999 to 2000, Lladró released models in homage to architect Antoni Gaudí, whose mosaic installations were inspired by undulating natural forms. *Left to right*, "In Barcelona" (#6664 G) and "Modernism" (#6665 G), retired in 2004. Sculptor: Joan Coderch. Courtesy of Joëlle Ley. $275–$300 ea.

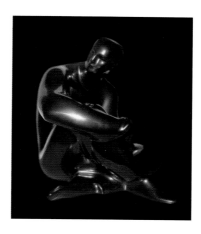

"Destiny (Ebony Look)" (#8279), retired in 2010 at a last retail price of $385. Lladró has always been an innovative company, working in modernistic designs as well as the traditional figural themes for which it is more broadly known. Sculptor: José Luis Santes. Courtesy of Jorge L. Gonzalez Rodriguez. $450–$525.

In 2016, the Lladró family announced that it had begun the process of selling its porcelain company. Later in this chapter, I'll be giving readers what is known about what led up to that decision and what it means for Lladró collecting. But even before that, Lladró had begun striking out in some new design directions, not all of which were universally welcomed even by those within the family.

NEW DESIGN DIRECTIONS

Lladró porcelain has continued to innovate—sometimes wildly! You can keep up with all the latest innovations on the company website, www.lladro.com. In this book, I want to mention just some of the highlights in new designs.

The company has enlisted the participation of several internationally famous designers in developing new product lines for decorative porcelain. In one sense, this is not an entirely new direction for Lladró: the company has enlisted the design expertise of famous artists from outside the company before. In the mid-1980s, Pablo Serrano did a series of studies of highly stylized head busts of Don Quixote, Don Quixote and Sancho Panza together, and their creator D. Miguel de Cervantes, as well as two full-figure studies, in various colors, of a stylized owl and of Isabel la Católica. In the 1990s, Enrique San Isidro had developed the incomparably wonderful and highly successful Goyescas line for Lladró.

Lladró today looks to artists such as Jaime Hayón and Bodo Sperlein because collaborating with known artists is a strategy that has worked for Lladró in the past. One might be tempted to conclude that the work of the new artists is edgier and more modernistic than anything previously undertaken in Lladró. But I imagine the Serrano studies looked pretty far out, too, nearly twenty-five years ago (and still look pretty wild today!).

What feels like a new era in edgy designs began in 2006 with the Re-Cyclos line, followed a year later by Re-Deco. Both lines were attempts to reinterpret, consistent with modern sensibilities and the interests of a younger market, some of the classic elements in Lladró's own history. Re-Cyclos took certain older porcelain models and put them together in new configurations. Re-Deco "deconstructed emblematic figurines and gave them a new decoration."[1] What that actually entailed, as it turns out, is taking some of the most popular figurines in

A sampling of first-series Lladró Christmas bells, of which I have the complete set of 10 made between 1987 and 1996. Bells such as these have been used in Lladró's new "Re-Cyclos" line to form spheres held together with metal clamps.

Bunnies sculpted by Fulgencio García, issued 1991, retired 1994, $80 last retail. *Left to right*: "Sleeping Bunny" (#5904 G), "Preening Bunny" (#5906 G), "Sitting Bunny" (#5907 G). Missing: "Attentive Bunny" (#5905 G). "Sitting Bunny" and "Attentive Bunny" were later reprised with platinum enhancement for the Re-Deco collection as model #s 7044 and 7043 respectively.

the historical catalog for Lladró and recasting them in white porcelain that has been either accented with platinum or decorated in color with matte and glossy surfaces combined in the same piece.

I confess that when Re-Cyclos first came out, I was nonplussed by it. One Re-Cyclos project took the company's spare inventory of Lladró Christmas bells and clamped them together with metal brackets to form a kind of decorative globe. Presumably, the source of the bells for that project was excess company inventory from the several years' worth of annual Christmas bells the company has produced. I guess the artistic vision here was that arranging the bells open-end-out with rims touching could eventually form a sphere if you could find a way to hold them in position. The bells are too heavy to do this with liquid porcelain or other adhesive. The metal clamp solution doesn't do much for me aesthetically, but to each his or her own aesthetic! Another project (by Bodo Sperlein) involved chandeliers made with hundreds of suspended Lladró butterflies, bells, or other elements—the largest chandelier of which will set a buyer back $120,000 USD as of this writing (and, yes, that's the correct number of zeros!).

When I heard about and saw photos of Re-Deco, I had a wave of déjà vu, a sense of Lladró having tried something similar before. Some years earlier, Lladró had brought out the Legend Collection, a line of white porcelain angels and other fantasy figures accented with gold, a series that never really caught on. What makes the Re-Deco effort different seems to be more than just a matter of decorative accent, platinum versus gold. Whereas the former effort invented models to go with the gold, Re-Deco reprises classic Lladró models with proven appeal in addition to some brand-new models—apparently, anything company artisans thought would look "pretty in platinum." In other words, whereas the Legend Collection may have strayed too far afield in letting the porcelain become secondary to the gold, the Re-Deco line tries to place the metallic enhancement at the service of known porcelain models.

“Morning Delivery” (#6398 G), retired in 2001. That year, the news wasn't good. With US headquarters in Manhattan, Lladró, too, suffered the global economic fallout from 9/11. In 2002, Lladró lost money for the first time in its history. Sculptor: José Luis Alvarez. Courtesy of Teresa K. Schmitt. $200–$225.

I'm not a great fan of platinum and gold enhancements. On the other hand, I find the color-variation items in the Re-Deco line (those that use shades of the same color of rose or blue or gray against a white surface in alternating matte and gloss) aesthetically stunning, compelling, and irresistible—a porcelain lover's dream.

In 2008, Lladró brought out "Love I—Blossoms" (#7231 G), "Love II—Blossoms" (#7232), and "Love III—Blossoms" (#7233 G), consisting of three different, more or less classically modeled Lladró couples, each covered with progressively more flowerwork (and, accordingly, ranging greatly in retail price from $640 to $7,000) until the heads are entirely covered with flowerwork in "Love II" and the entire torsos of both figures in "Love III." The official Lladró website describes these reconfigurations as "evocative, poetic creations with a touch of humor."[2] Such restyling of older products seemed to be aimed toward a wealthier and more avant-garde clientele than what has traditionally been Lladró's consumer base. According to press reports of the time, Lladró representatives said this approach seemed to be working for the company, albeit slowly.[3]

Another initiative is being called "High Porcelain"—as in *haute couture* (high fashion) or *haute cuisine*. This line markets the most complicated of recent Lladró porcelain groupings, those most aesthetically and technically challenging to make. Some of the more difficult pieces are also those most likely to appeal to international markets: "Queen of the Nile" (model #1918, issued in 2006 in a very limited edition of only 100) for a Middle Eastern market, for example, or "Great Dragon" (#1933, in an only slightly larger edition of 150) for an Asian market.

All three of these initiatives (Re-Cyclos, Re-Deco, and High Porcelain) have several components in common. First, they are aimed at new markets—specifically new international markets with an aesthetically sophisticated clientele of modernist tastes. Second, they are aimed at an upscale, exclusive, and affluent clientele. ("Red Dragon," in the High Porcelain line, retired in 2010, retailed at $25,000 and is offered at $30,000 as of this writing on Janet Hammer's website, and "Queen of the Nile" is just retiring in 2018 at a staggering $200,000, up from $150,000 when it was first issued in 2006.) Third, they are meant to garner respect for Lladró on the international cultural scene. The fact that several renowned and respected designers (Bodo Sperlein, the *Committee* group, and Jaime Hayón) have been associated with these initiatives has already earned Lladró some measure of the critical respect and acclaim that has sometimes eluded the company as journalists indiscriminately tossed around the rote slur "kitsch" in referring to Lladró models in more-traditional themes. Finally, in appealing to new markets, the three new lines built on known strengths within the Lladró corpus.

NOT ENOUGH TO KEEP THE BUSINESS IN THE FAMILY

By the year 2000, Lladró had become very nearly a conglomerate, with corporate interests in real estate, finance, and energy sectors. It had also acquired the prestigious Carrera Jewelry Company.

But as it was for so many other expansionist companies, the first decade of the twenty-first century was a difficult one for Lladró. September 11, 2001 saw the first major blow to the global economy when markets stalled in the wake of the terrorist attack on the World Trade Center as a symbol of global commercial power. September 11 seems to have hit Lladró harder and had a more lasting effect than it had on some other companies, perhaps because the headquarters for Lladró's US division is located in Manhattan. The devaluation of the US dollar and subsequent downturns in the stock market also had a negative effect on Lladró, whose strongest export market was the United States. More recently, Spain has had its own economic challenges, and this certainly has not helped Lladró's bottom line.

In 2002, the Lladró company actually lost money for the first time in its history. Throughout most of the rest of that decade, a succession of labor negotiations that included worker concessions on shortened workweeks and even layoffs, carefully negotiated not only with labor unions but also with the Spanish government, became necessary to keep the company solvent.

The three aging Lladró founders had already turned the management of the company over to the second generation of the family by the late 1990s. As reported in Spanish press accounts of the ensuing years, the cousins couldn't agree on a direction for the company, and the disputes became sufficiently fractious that in 2007, the decision was made to break the company up and divide its commercial interests among the three branches of the family. The eldest founder, Juan Lladró, along with his children, ran the porcelain and jewelry interests, while José's family ran the real estate and Vicente's family had controlling interests in Lladró's financial entities and renewable-energy projects.

Throughout this period, it was difficult to get information about what was actually happening within the company, but what is clear from Spanish-language media interviews with the youngest founding brother, Vicente Lladró, is that a kind of perpetual company reorganization was ongoing. On one level, this division seemed a nearly catastrophic outcome for a company that has built its fortunes on a reputation for family solidarity. However, we now know through José Lladró's memoir, *Passenger of Life*, published in 2002, that family tensions were present in the company even from its earlier days.

On the other hand, healthy companies are companies that can adapt, sometimes radically, and what had in recent years become a porcelain *division* plagued by family divisions might have developed a certain forward momentum once it became a porcelain *company* with one branch of the family in charge. (Actually, the Juan Lladrós own 70% of the porcelain company, with the other two families sharing equally in the remaining 30%.) There seems to have been a consensus, both within the company itself and among outside analysts, that the former

Issued in 1982, Gres "Watching the Dove" (#3526), still retailing more than 35 years later despite its $960 retail price. Maybe Vicente Lladró is on to something about the tastes of the collector base! Lladró's challenge remains finding its optimal mix of innovative and traditional designs. Courtesy of Joëlle Ley.

"Passion and Soul" (#8683 G) was issued in 2013 for the company's 60th anniversary (so indicated on the base), tracing back to the company's founding year, 1953. Model style harks back to Lladró's earliest designs. Sculptor: José Luis Santes. Courtesy of Teresa K. Schmitt. Current retail: $945.

Porcelanas Lladró had rested too long on its laurels, failing to anticipate changes in consumer tastes in its primary export markets while, at the same time, neglecting to develop new export markets in burgeoning economies such as those of China and India. More recently, Lladró Porcelain had been at last responding proactively to these challenges and opportunities by further enhancing its reputation for innovative design and by reaching out to emerging global markets.

But apparently these innovative ventures weren't enough or were too late to buoy the company's flagging fortunes. According to one Spanish-language report (which I have here translated into English), "In any event, so much stress caused by flagging sales and the tensions within the family weren't doing the well-known porcelain firm any good."[4] At least one of the founding brothers, Vicente, felt the new direction and its product price hikes were placing Lladró porcelains out of reach of its traditional and most loyal customer base. In interviews, Vicente blamed this straying from its roots for the company's financial decline leading to its forced sale in 2017.[5]

In the end, the family itself agreed that something had to give, and that a sale of the company was the only option for its survival. In December 2016, an emotional Juan Lladró announced to his employees that the porcelain company would be sold to PHI Industrial. In a December 2016 interview, Vicente Lladró was said at last to have approved of the company's sale to PHI, of which he had been sharply critical in an earlier October piece,[6] even though he "would not have sold it for all the money in the world" (Vicente had not participated in the sale negotiations).[7]

The new owner, which had recently also acquired the US company Proctor and Gamble, has something of a reputation as a "turnaround" entity for the struggling brands it acquires. The new owner has assured Lladró employees and consumers that it will retain the Lladró brand name, which PHI says it considers the major asset in this acquisition, and that it will maintain Lladró's production staff and facilities in Tavernes Blanques.[8]

The sole tangible asset of the porcelain company that remains in family control is the real-estate interests, including Porcelain City itself; PHI acquires the brand and the staff that makes it and will rent the factory facilities from the Lladrós.[9]

THE FUTURE OF THE NAO BRAND: AN OPEN QUESTION

As noted, the Lladró company had learned its lesson about the trade-offs demanded of the company whenever it failed to include the Lladró name in the marks of its other brands, among which NAO is today the only survivor. Hence, Lladró has, for many years, taken care to include the words "by Lladró" in its NAO mark.

I was surprised, then, when I noticed that the streamlined mark on the most recent models drops altogether the attribution to Lladró. "Autumn Stroll" (NAO #1232) was retired sometime after 2012, but before the sale of the Lladró company to PHI. The loss of Lladró attribution in the NAO mark may indicate that the family had already, even before the sale of the Lladró company itself, begun contemplating the option of spinning NAO off as a separate company to sink or swim on its own.

For all the confusion it may initially have caused for marketing, NAO has also been a cash cow for the Lladró family—and it is unclear that this subsidiary brand was even included in the sale to PHI. Should the family have decided beforehand to carve NAO out of any sale of the main company, this could be another reason for the decision to stop including the Lladró name in the NAO mark. In any event, it will be fascinating to see what shakes out for the future of the NAO brand.

WHAT DOES ALL THIS MEAN FOR LLADRÓ COLLECTORS?

Where do these new directions—and especially the new ownership—leave those of us, whether veteran Lladró collectors or collectors just starting out? In the first place, whatever enhances the reputation and prestige of retail production in Lladró also enhances, by power of association, the reputation and prestige of Lladró on the secondary market. In the decorative arts, people do respond to the cachet associated with famous names.

New design initiatives build on traditional strengths of the company, including some of its traditional models. This could well mean that as a result of their exposure to newer and more-edgy configurations of traditional Lladró themes, upscale collectors will also take a second look at older, more traditional and classic designs and develop a new appreciation for them. As Vicente Lladró himself has pointed out, the real strength, beauty, and longevity of the Lladró corpus is in these older, more classic forms.[10]

The addition of precious-metal veneers to porcelain isn't, the company has insisted, just for those who enjoy ostentation in their decor. The decoration is said to add sculptural depth to the surfaces of the white porcelain models. Still, there's a point at which added decoration can begin to look more like decadence than aesthetic enhancement. Many sophisticated arts connoisseurs feel that less is more, and they may well tire of the platinum and turquoise and extravagant floral embellishments on the newer configurations and turn instead to the relatively unembellished appearance of the original models.

Alternatively, the newer designs could generate a more permanent market that is relatively distinct from Lladró's traditional collector base. That would mean that the secondary market in traditional Lladró porcelains would consist of two pretty much independent pools of collectors, one of which would be left relatively free to indulge its passion for the more traditional Lladró designs. In the US as

"Autumn Stroll" (NAO #1232 G) was issued in 1996 and retired sometime after 2010 at a last retail price of $129. In this and other recent issues, the name "Lladró" appears nowhere in the mark—a fact that invites speculation as to future plans for this brand. $150–$175.

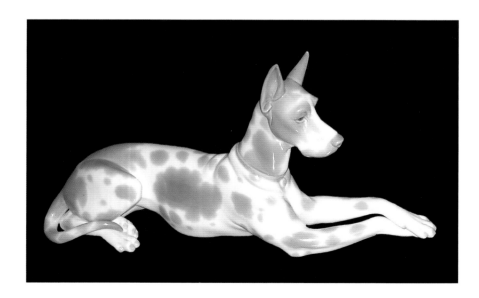

Lladró's "Great Dane" (#1068 G), retired in 1989 at a last retail of $380. Recently, Lladró has been experimenting with a more stylized and modernistic approach to its animal models, as seen, for instance, in its Balance Collection. Sculptor: Juan Huerta. Courtesy of Jorge L. Gonzalez Rodriguez. $500–$550

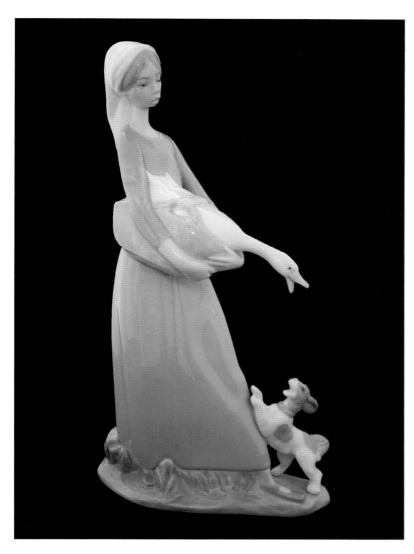

Fulgencio García's trademark elongated style was once itself considered avant-garde. Today, rural-themed figurines such as "Girl with Goose and Dog" (#4866 G/M), issued in 1974 and retired in 1993, are often undervalued on the secondary market. But they're destined to be rediscovered and better appreciated. $175–$200.

elsewhere, as the organic-food movement gains ground and as family farms and rural areas continue to be eaten up by urban and suburban sprawl, Lladró's pastoral and farming models may also acquire a profound nostalgia appeal for current and future collectors.

As for the change in ownership, consolidation has been a recent trend in many industries, including porcelain collectibles. Beswick, for example, is now owned by Royal Doulton, Wedgwood has acquired Crown Staffordshire, Rosenthal bought out Hutschenreuther, and so on. There is no evidence that this consolidation has had any negative effect on the porcelain brands mentioned, all of which have retained their names and distinctive identities. There is no reason to expect the same won't also be true of Lladró. Although the Lladró company has not been acquired by another porcelain maker, it clearly needed a new owner that could turn the company around in a manner that another porcelain group probably could not. Aside from that, the sale was necessary. Consensus of business and industry experts is that inadequate succession planning and preparation at Lladró had left the second-generation family members in no real position to run the company successfully. [11]

Acknowledging all that, and quite aside from the impact of the company's sale outside the family that created it, collectors who recognized the importance of Lladró before the rest of the world did are now aging and even passing away. They have sometimes found that their children do not share their interest in Lladró. Finding new ways to generate secondary-market "buzz" for the original lines of Lladró porcelain is as crucial to the health of the Lladró secondary market as new design directions have been crucial for attracting newer and even more upscale retail markets. What collectors have going for them is an abiding interest in Lladró, which keeps coming to the top of collecting consciousness like cream in a milk jug. I hope this book will be one catalyst for that effort to infuse new vigor into Lladró collecting and the Lladró secondary market.

CHAPTER 8

FREQUENTLY ASKED QUESTIONS ABOUT LLADRÓ COLLECTING

How important is it to the value of a Lladró to have the original box?

The answer is not at all: cardboard and packing straw are not collectible. The Lladró brothers themselves have repeatedly said that the value of Lladró porcelains is irrespective of their original shipping containers. Think about it; how many pieces of eighteenth-century English Stafford-shire would still have their original packaging? How about a four-teenth-century Ming vase?

Boxes in decent condition are nice to have for storing and moving Lladró in as safe a manner as possible, but even that advantage is lost over time. Eventually, the boxes themselves (especially those made in the 1980s or earlier) deteriorate to such an extent that they offer next to no protection for the item and may just as well be discarded. Even when the boxes are in good condition, they don't lend themselves to breaking down for flat storage when empty and, therefore, take up a lot of space.

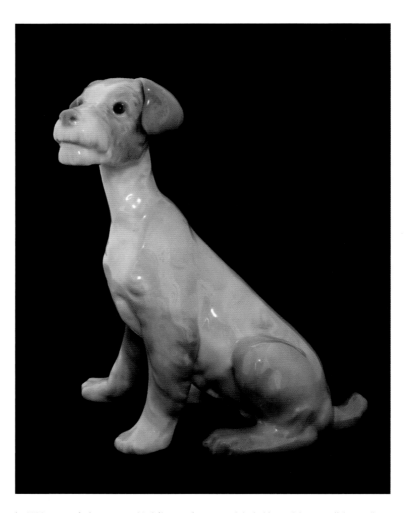

In 1981, many of what are now Lladró's most famous and desirable models went off the retail market, including "Setter" (#4583 G/M). When I found it in an antique shop for $168, it didn't have its original box. Ask me if I cared! Sculptor: Fulgencio García. $275–$350.

I have a Lladró that I think must be a rare variant of the one in the Lladró official catalogs. Mine is a mirror image of the cataloged model; everything in the photo that's on the right on mine is on the left in the photo and vice versa. How much is my rare variant worth?

Sorry to burst the bubble, but Lladró sometimes mistakenly published its catalog negatives backward. What you have is the actual model; what's in the catalog photo is also the actual model shown in a reverse-printed negative.

The colors in my Lladró are a lot more subdued than those in the catalog photos. Is mine a "second"?

Most cameras rely on color and color variations as one of their focus points. When colors are as subdued as they are in Lladró, many modern cameras will try to "correct" for this, even in official catalog photos, by making the colors appear darker or more vibrant than they actually are. Consequently, photos are notoriously unreliable in judging the actual color of an item (the better the camera or the photographer, of course, the less color discrepancy there will be between item and image).

Aside from photography challenges, Lladró is, in every important sense, handmade, and that means that there will be minor variations in the underglaze painting from example to example of the same model. Some of the examples will appear more vibrant in their color than others, and there may be slight variations in expression in the facial painting.

There's a tiny hole in the base of my Lladró, and I can hear a rattling sound when I shake it. Is it damaged?

The little hole and the pinging sound you noted are normal. The factory makes the hole in the base of every one of its figurines prior to firing to allow steam to escape from the model so that it doesn't explode in the kiln. The instrument used to make the hole punches inward, which displaces a little "plug" of porcelain into the interior of the figurine; this tiny bit of porcelain hardens along with the rest of the figurine during firing and makes that little rattling sound inside the hollow figurine.

You seem really down on items with altered marks. Why shouldn't I buy a second or a gray-market Lladró, especially when I can get them so much cheaper than full price?

It depends on what you want out of your collection. If all you want are a few elegant porcelain pieces to spread around your living quarters to impress the neighbors when they come in to borrow a cup of sugar or one of your tools, then seconds will get the job done. But if you're trying to build a first-class collection of interest to other collectors, you won't get there buying seconds and gray-market items with logo scrapes. Within the collector market for Lladró, a second will not command either the interest or the resale price of a first-quality item with an unaltered mark, because knowledgeable collectors won't touch cataloged items with altered logos.

"Little Friskies" (Lladró #5032 G/M), issued in 1979; matte retired in 1991, glazed in 1997. Because Lladró colors are so neutral, some cameras may compensate, in their search for clear focus points, by making colors seem darker than they really are. Sculptor: Jan Huerta. $275–$300, slightly more for the matte.

"A Warm Welcome" (Lladró model #6903 G), currently available retail for $550. If all you want is a nice decoration for your den, a logo-altered purchase will do the job, but if you intend to build a serious collection, you'll want more from your marks. Sculptor: Ernest Massuet.

NAO "Girl with Ducks" (NAO #26 G/M)—a misnomer both in English and Spanish since there's only one duck! She has an impressed NAO mark with other artisan marks, including an etched "16"—note: not the model number. Matte retired 1991, glazed 1998, last retail $115. Sculptor: Vicente Martinez. $125–$150.

"Clean-Up Time" (Lladró #4838 G) was first issued in 1973, before Lladró began copyrighting its figurines. But she was on the retail market until 1993, so later firings would have the copyright notice added—and, no, her name's not "DAISA"! Sculptor: Julio Fernandez. $250–$275.

There are a lot of hand-etched and machine-stamped marks and numbers on the base of my Lladró/NAO/Zaphir. What do all these numbers and marks mean, and which of them is the model number?

Lladró didn't begin stamping model numbers into the base of its brands until the mid-1980s. Consequently, nothing produced prior to that time will have a serial number on the base. Most of the hand-etched marks on the base of every item made in a Lladró brand are the marks of various artisans who worked on the piece; they are used for internal quality tracking during manufacture and are part of the handmade charm of Lladró porcelains, but they have no significance for identifying particular models.

The most commonly seen machine stamp on the base consists of a series of numbers and letters that appear to be a date-of-production code. I've been able to determine that the last two items in the code refer to the day and month of production. The first letter is either a year date code or a batch code that I haven't been able to crack. So, for example, if the date on the bottom of your piece says B-14 F, it means that the item was fired on the 14th of February—which, if Valentine's Day happens to be important to you, could be a fun factoid to know. The month code, by the way, uses the Spanish names for the months, so something that says D-29 E was fired on the 29th of January (the Spanish word for which is *enero*).

What does the word "DAISA" mean in a Lladró mark? Is it the name of my lady figurine?

DAISA is an acronym that stands for Diseños Artísticos e Industriales, Sociedad Anónimo (the last two letters, SA for Sociedad Anónimo, function in much the same way as the suffixes "Inc." in the US and "Ltd." in the UK). DAISA is the name of the business entity within the Lladró company that owns its design and copyrights. Its acronym was first incorporated into the mark around 1977, the year Lladró began copyrighting its designs. Items produced prior to that year will not have the acronym in the mark. On the other hand, since the acronym is unique to Lladró, no mark that has DAISA in it can be anything other than a Lladró product, so it serves as one way that a collector can determine whether an unusual later item that doesn't have the Lladró name in the brand mark is actually a Lladró product.

The date in the mark of my figurine says 1977, but I know this figurine was made much earlier than that. What's up?

Under growing pressure from stylistic imitators, not to mention actual counterfeits, Lladró finally began copyrighting its models in 1977. Anything fired after that year will have a date next to the DAISA acronym, but this is only the date the item was copyrighted, not the year it was issued. For older models that were marketed prior to 1977, only those actually fired after the copyright was established will have the copyright date in the mark, and all those early models still in production at the time the copyright was established will have the same year, 1977, in the mark as copyright "year 1."

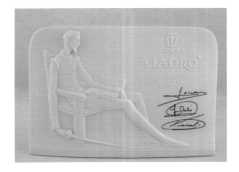

This was the membership premium given to all first-time members of the Lladró Collectors Society. One of the few uses I've ever found for it is as a signature identifier for figurine models signed by one of the three founding brothers.

I have a signed piece, but I can't tell which family member's signature it is. Assuming I could find out, how much more would my item be worth than an unsigned piece?

Spanish signatures tend to be florid and elaborate, so it would, indeed, be difficult to determine who signed a Lladró figurine if we didn't have some help. Fortunately, the Lladró brothers signed a plaque that was produced for the Lladró Collectors Society (before that organization was closed down), and one of the few uses I've been able to find for this ornament is those signatures. Comparing them to what's on the base of yours, you'd be able to tell if the signature is that of one of the three founding brothers, the oldest of whom is, as of this writing, in his nineties. At present, however, the market doesn't currently recognize a value enhancement for hand-signed Lladró. When that generation passes, those original signatures *may* command a price premium.

One of the reasons it's hard to know for sure what future cachet a founder signature may have is that the Lladró family members, from the founders through the second generation, have done hundreds of signing events over the years, so a signature isn't all that unusual. As far as the history of porcelain arts is concerned, the mark *was* considered the signature in centuries past, and people didn't expect porcelain to be "enhanced" with hand signatures by family members at special signing (read: marketing) events. By the time the second-generation Lladró family members had begun to sign pieces, the relationship between family member and the actual production of the item being signed had become pretty far removed—as opposed, for example, to having the sculptor who developed the model sign it, which seems to have happened only in the Zaphir line.

I bought a limited edition Lladró on the secondary market that originally came with a wooden base, but mine doesn't have it. Does this affect the value?

This situation is somewhat analogous to the question about original boxes. Logically, it shouldn't affect the value because the base is wooden and presumably replaceable (by a skilled carpenter if not by the manufacturer). That is, it is not integral to the porcelain model itself. (See next question for more on this.)

My limited-edition Lladró came with a detachable wooden base. Should I glue the two together somehow so that they won't become separated?

Don't do it! You'll create enormous problems for yourself in any future need to demonstrate authenticity of the piece; the glued-on base will obscure the authenticity marks on the porcelain underside, and the attached wood would not

Angel tree topper "Angelic Melody" (Lladró #5963 G), an annual limited edition in 1993. This one is signed by José Lladró and dated 11/93—nice to have, but not a value enhancer, at least not at this point in time. Sculptor: Francisco Catalá. $200–$250—with or without the signature.

One of Lladró's large and expensive limited editions, "Valencian Couple on Horse" (#1472 G), retired in 2001 at last retail of $1,550. It had a total edition size of 3,000. Sculptor: Juan Huerta. Courtesy of Teresa K. Schmitt. $2,000–$2,500.

The base of "Valencian Couple on Horse," giving us the following information: authentic Lladró mark, sculptor name (Juan Huerta), decorator (V. Navarro), and item number 141 in the limited edition of 3,000. Why glue a wooden base to this at the expense of access to the authenticating information?

be easy to remove without damaging the porcelain, the marks, or both. Better to risk losing the base, which is not integral to the model, than to lose the ability to readily authenticate the porcelain.

I can't find my Lladró figurine anywhere on the internet. Does that mean it's rare?

No, it just means you haven't been able to find it on the internet. I get this question a lot in email traffic generated from my website, www.elportalporcelana.info. On the basis of the number of times the item in question has been photo-listed right there in my information web catalog or in Janet Hammer's comprehensive web catalog for core collection Lladró on her website A Retired Collection (www.aretiredcollection.com), I've learned to take the claim that "it isn't anywhere on the internet" with a grain of salt.

It is certainly true that there are unusual and uncataloged Lladró items to be found on the secondary market; that's part of what makes Lladró collecting so much fun! But in many, if not most, cases in which someone "can't find it anywhere on the internet," the problem is a deficient search strategy.

I have a porcelain model marked "Made in Spain" and with a [fill in the blank] logo/name that was given to me by an aunt who bought it when she was traveling in Spain. Is this a Lladró? What is its model number and name, and how much is it worth?

By far, the most frequent question I get is from noncollectors who happen upon my website in their search for information about non-Lladró products. So here are the short answers to this multilayered question. First, I'm reasonably confident that I've identified in this book all the brands actually owned by or at any time affiliated with Lladró, so if the item has a mark at all but it is not one of the marks featured in this book, it is not a Lladró brand.

Second, because these non-Lladró companies, most of them working "in the Lladró style," are generally fairly small and have no retail or collector catalogs, it's really impossible to identify the model name or number or when it was made.

Finally, values on porcelain figurines by famous companies such as Lladró, Royal Doulton, or Royal Copenhagen are driven by collector familiarity and demand, so brands that lack this familiarity and demand have no tested market value. These factors are the case even with Nadal, the best of these non-Lladró companies in terms of the quality of its products: an inability to identify the figurines severely dampens serious collector interest in them.

If the item is well enough made and reflects a popular subject, such as animals, clowns, or ballerinas, it may be able to command attention in its own right. In such a case, the value is what someone would be willing to pay for it, and that can be tested only by prices achieved for that or a similar item on the actual secondary market (e.g., at consignment to a secondary-market shop, live auction, or internet auction).

APPENDIX

1: Some Authentic Lladró Brand Marks

Some of the marks shown here are crisper than others, depending on how deeply the marks were impressed or how the backstamps unfurled in the kiln. Extra etched marks appearing in some of the photos (e.g., a star or a sunset or a diamond) are production etchings from artisans who worked on the piece, and were used for quality tracking—and probably also as a means for various artisans to assert internal bragging rights on items that passed muster as first quality. Some photos show the blowhole in the base if it's very near the mark; a hole like this occurs on every Lladró piece and is a means for steam to escape during firing so that the model doesn't blow up in the kiln.

Early etched "Lladró España" mark (ca. late 1950s) with the country of origin (in Spanish) faintly visible. Items on which this mark appears would not have been made for export to the US, since the McKinley Tariff Act requires country-of-origin names be in English.

Machine-impressed "Lladró España" mark (1960) with paper label added, sufficient to pass muster with US Customs. Occasionally, one sees a mark from the early 1960s that says "Espain," a Spanglish misspelling accounted for by the fact that there are few, if any, Spanish-language nouns that begin with the letter *S*.

Etched "Lladró Made in Spain" with artisan marks (ca. 1962).

First Lladró backstamp (mid- to late 1960s), lacking the accent over the *o*, leading to widespread mispronunciation of the name with the accent on the first syllable instead of where it belongs, on the second.

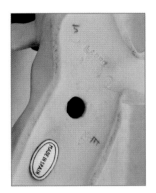

Next iteration of the backstamp (early 1970s), with the missing accent added along with the "registered" symbol (®) and the DAISA acronym for Diseños Artísticos e Industriales, S.A., Lladró's design rights entity.

Blue backstamp with DAISA copyright (first used in 1977), showing heavy "bleeding" around the edges, a risk in growing complexity of the mark and the need to limit the space it occupies on the base.

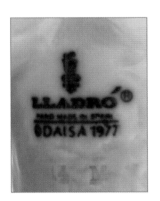

Streamlined mark beginning in the 1990s, with simplified bellflower logo and crisper lettering.

Most recent Lladró mark with a registration number (not to be confused with the model number), unique to each model (in this case, LHF 33). The addition was intended as an authenticity enhancement and has no meaning for model identification.

Lladró Collectors Society figurine mark, with impressed model number, for "It Wasn't Me."

Company mark with an added stamp for "Event Figurines."

Oldest, impressed NAO mark (ca. late 1950s–late '60s) with an artisan's "star" mark.

First NAO brown backstamp, no logo (ca. 1970 to mid-'70s).

NAO backstamp with first ship logo and the all-important attribution "by Lladró," ca. 1975).

NAO mark with multiple registration/copyright symbols and copyright date added (first used for a 1977 copyright date and used through the 1980s).

Streamlined 1990s NAO backstamp with entirely different typeface in name, ship logo integrated into the last letter of the name, and somewhat lighter brown color in the stamp.

Latest iteration of the NAO mark, with yet again a different typeface for the name, ship detached from the last letter of the name—and a step backward in attribution in which Lladró appears nowhere in the mark.

Hispania backstamp with the DAISA notice, which is the only clue to the brief era of Lladró's ownership of the brand.

Zaphir's scripted mark, clearly showing how that first letter could be taken for an *L* and the last for an *n*.

First Golden Memories mark with logo (1992 copyright date for a 1991 issue) but no attribution to Lladró.

Second iteration of the Golden Memories mark (1993 for a 1992 issue date), with the attribution "From the Lladró Family of Products."

SOME ODD BUT GENUINE MARKS

The NAO backstamp in cobalt blue (ca. 1960s), probably a very brief intervening mark between the earlier impressed mark and the first backstamp in brown.

An example of a double mark on the base of a seated Lladró angel, a production "mistake" that doesn't affect value of the item, one way or the other.

A NAO mark over a scraped-off darker logo that may well have been a Lladró blue backstamp.

APPENDIX

2: Lladró Sculptors

The sculptors listed in the first part of this appendix worked on Lladró at some point from the inception of the company through the 1990s. With few exceptions, these sculptors, whose names were famously associated with the core Lladró brand, also sculpted most of the NAO models, and some of them also worked on Zaphir. They are listed in alphabetical order by the first letter of the surname.

JOSÉ LUIS ALVAREZ

Alvarez produced the single unicorn models found in the Lladró corpus: #s 5826 G, 5880 G, 5993 G. Also produced a whimsical series of Easter rabbits (#s 5886–5889 G, *illus. p. 67*). His incomparable "Pas de Deux" ballet piece (#6374 G) is a work so technically proficient and so consummately graceful that it serves as an iconic model of what makes a Lladró a Lladró.

AMPARO AMADOR

This name, along with that of Fulgencio García, is connected with some of the earliest recorded Lladró works of the 1950s (e.g., "young Ballerina" [#213.08 G] and "Little Gypsy" [#0214.08]) but then drops out of the record.

ANTONIO ARNAL

Another very early name in the history of Lladró, producing only a handful of models in white porcelain in the period 1956–58: "Hunting Lamp (#0076.05 G), "Girl with Pitcher" (#0118.06 G), "Girl with Flower Basket" (#0026.09 M), "The Prom" (#0212.04 G), "Grace" (#0244.10 G).

ANTONIO BALLESTER

Noted especially for his bird models (*illus. p. 51*), including the spectacular "Forest" (#1243 G), featuring small birds amid a flowering bush with great poms of individually fashioned flowers, and "Ducks at the Pond" (#1317 G), as well as his famous Gres limited-edition groupings of "Turtle Doves" (#s 3519 and 3520). Ballester's difficult-to-find "Swan" (#4829 G/M) manages, in its stylized form, to express the essence of this graceful bird.

FRANCISCO CATALÁ

Among his works were the annual Christmas treetop angels produced in the 1990s (*illus. p. 71, 148*). He also sculpted the wonderful "Swan with Wings Spread" (#5231 G, *illus. p. 65*) and its companion piece "Graceful Swan" (#5230 G). Among his most famous complex groupings were "Jockey with Lady" (#5036 G) and the still-retailing limited-edition "18th Century Coach" (#1485 G).

JOAN CODERCH

One of less than a handful of female sculptors in Lladró's stable—and for many years the only one—Coderch was recently joined by Begoña Jauregui and Virginia González. She did the majority of the individual models of sports players for Lladró: #s6090–6091 G, 6107–6108 G, and 6135 G, as well as the spectacular "To the Rim" (#1800), an intensely lively grouping of basketball players leaping for the basket. Coderch is also interested in classic myths and fantasies, producing for Lladró the stunning limited-edition "Pegasus" (#1778 G), retired in 1996 (*illus. p. 30*). She also designed several of the models in Lladró's "Black Legacy" line of African American themes, such as "My New Pet" (#5549 G); a series of elegant ladies in evening dress (#s 6180–6182 G); and "Delicate Bundle" (#6167 G). Her gorgeous "Graceful Ballet" (#6240 G) is among Lladró's most lovely and aerodynamic models. Also did a series of Lladró tribute models honoring the work of architect Antoni Gaudí (*illus. p. 136*).

SALVADOR DEBÓN

Among his most famous works are "Swans Take Flight" (#5912 G), "Gypsy Woman with Bear" (#4919 G), and limited editions featuring antique cars: "Car in Trouble" (#1375 G), "Young Couple with Car" (#1393 G), "A Sunday Drive" (#1510 G). He did many of the Lladró models featuring Japanese women and girls in traditional dress (*illus. p. 56*), including the fabulous "Oriental Garden" (#1775 G, a limited edition still in production). His work wasn't all sweetness and light, however, as illustrated by the danger and urgency conveyed in his Gres limited-edition "Rescue" (#3504). He also designed the series of Zodiac figures (#s 6214–6225 G, *illus. p. 57*).

JULIO FERNANDEZ

Sculpted several of Lladró's early animal and bird models: hens and rooster (#s 1041–1043 G/M), large and small hippos (#s 1044–1045 G/M), ram and ewe (#s 1046–1047 G/M), wild ducks (#s 1056–1057 G, *illus. p. 42*), an afghan hound (#1069), and a famous series of three "Beagle Puppies" (#s 1070–1072 G/M, *illus. p. 60*). Created most of the large Asian-themed vases in the Lladró line. Also sculpted the pieces in Lladró's famous chess set (#4833 G).

SALVADOR FURIÓ

Known for his dignified portrayals of historical, literary, and religious figures. Also created some of the darker-themed limited editions for Lladró, such as the deer hunts in #s 1238 G, 1377 G, 4880 G. His style was in many respects the most classical and representational of all the Lladró sculptors, but his skill and attention to historical detail produced consummate work. Perhaps his most famous and emblematic model is "Don Quixote" (#1030 G/M). My own favorite examples of his work are "Little Flower Seller" (#5082 G) and "Chestnut Seller" (#1373 G). Although much of Furió's work was dignified and serious, he was also eminently capable of humor in his work, as in the wonderful grouping "Happy Drinkers" (#4956 G), the whimsical "Gardener in Trouble" (#4852 G/M), and a series of elongated clowns (#5762–5765 G).

FULGENCIO GARCÍA (D)

One of Lladró's earliest collaborators and most prolific sculptors and, as much as anyone else, responsible for the innovation that became a distinctively elongated Lladró style. At times a contentious collaborator, García created many of the most iconic models in the Lladró line: "Centaur Girl" (#1012 G), "Centaur Boy" (#1013 G), the three large models of the kings astride horses that the Lladró brothers famously gave to John Paul II (#s 1018–1020 M), "Sad Harlequin" (#4558 G/M), "Soccer Players" (limited-edition #1266 G, retired in 1986), and "Before the Dance" (a tableau of several ballerinas in waiting, #5972 G), among others. His "Shot on Goal" (#5879 G), with its wonderfully extended lines, is one of the most technically brilliant models in the Lladró line. Was intimately involved in the evolution of the NAO brand and created many of its earliest models, including several models known to have been produced at one time or other both in NAO and the core Lladró brands (*illus. p. 12–13, 37, 92, 109*). García died in December 1994 at the age of 79.

JUAN HUERTA

Works primarily in themes involving children with animals *(illus. pp. 27, 33, 49, 74–75, 77–78, 81, 83)*. Produced the famous Lladró sports puppets (#s 4966–4971 G). Sculpted the popular Days of the Week series of children, male and female (#s 6011–6024 G, *illus. p. 76*) and the popular and diffi-cult-to-find early "Santa" models (#s 4904 and 4905 G), retired in 1978. Also sculpted many of Lladró's animal models *(illus. p. 52, 58, 62, 65, 69, 103, 142)*, including the dynamic grouping "Attentive Dogs" (#4957 G), retired in 1981; "Pups in a Box" (#1121 G), retired in 1978; and three very small and very expensive dalmatian puppies (#s 1260–1262 G/M). Perhaps his most-famous animal models compose Lladró's earliest forays into animal caricature: the Painful Animals series (#s 5018–5023 G), produced from 1978 to 1981, featuring various animals sporting bandages or slings on parts of their bodies, and the passing-strange dog musician series (#s 1152–1156 G). He also created Lladró's Child Nativity set (#s 4670–4680 G/M, *illus. p. 32–33*) and the famous first model in the Lladró Collectors Society figurine series Members Only, "Little Pals" (#7600 G).

BEGOÑA JAUREGUI

A relatively recent addition (1997) to the Lladró sculptor stable and one of its few female sculptors, Jauregui did the "Kitty Surprise" (#6616 G), "Puppy Surprise" (6617 G), and "Fawn Surprise" (#6619 G) *(illus. p. 24)* eggs, whose tops lift off to reveal the animal surrounded by flowerwork inside. In 2009 and 2010, she did a pair of highly stylized ewe and ram sheep pairs in white and black colors, respectively, all of which were retired in 2013. She is also a sculptor of record for the NAO brand.

R. LOZANO

This sculptor's name appears only sporadically in Lladró model records. Worked on a few figurines in Lladró's Black Legacy series, including a series of child jazz musicians (#s 5832–5834 G). Also the sculptor of record for "Minstrel's Love" (#5821 G).

VICENTE MARTINEZ

One of Lladró's earliest collaborators, whose first model for them was "Pheasant" (#0331.13). Created several of Lladró's models of birds with flowers (#s 1298–1303 and 1368–1371 G). Also produced several centerpieces for Lladró: the two Girl's Head series in Gres (#s 1106–1109 and 2041–2042) and the bird and fish figural centerpiece series (#s 4692–4695). Sculpted the hard-to-find Percheron horse models (#s 4861–4863 G), which were produced only from 1974 to 1978. Sculpted a series of elegant women in 1920s costume (#s 5174–5176 G/M). Was also the sculptor for the famous "Egyptian Cat" models (#s 2130 in Gres and 5154 G in the regular porcelain formula). My hands-down favorite model by Martinez, though, is a work of outrageous whimsy, "Cow with Pig" (#4640 G/M), in which a large cow turns her head to look down upon a pig copping a meal from her udder. He also created one of NAO's most famous models, "Dancer with Veil" (#185 G), which, despite its early model number, is still in production today.

FRANCISCO POLOPE

Polope was particularly fond of fantasy themes and produced most of the Lladró Disney models, including Snow White and each of her Seven Dwarfs; "Tinkerbell" (#7518 G), sold at a Disney convention; and one of the largest and most expensive limited editions Lladró ever made, the colossal "Cinderella's Arrival" (#1785 and still in production at a current retail price of $33,000 USD). In the 1990s, he also produced some whimsical fantasy pieces that combined pets and flowers with shoes (*illus. p. 64*) and some that coupled elfin figures with large-petal flowerwork *(illus. p. 83)*, as well as the limited-edition "Easter Fantasy" (#1810 G).

JOSÉ PUCHE

Puche's sculpting interests are wide ranging. He is fond of girl models with big skirts, including the limited-edition "La Menina" (#1812 G, not yet sold out), #s 5518–5121 G, and #s 5410 and 6315 G. He also contributed high-style models such as "Lady of Nice" (#6213 G), "Lady of Monaco" (#6236 G), and "Afternoon Tea" (#1428 G/M, *illus. p. 81*). On a completely different thematic note, he did a series of child clowns (#s 5277–5279 G/M). Perhaps his loveliest creation for Lladró was the Gres limited-edition bust "Gentle Moment" (#3564, *illus. p. 79*), featuring a girl with large flowers in her hair, nuzzling the head of a horse. Among his most famous works are the series of schoolgirls each holding an outsized vowel letter (#s 5145–5149 G) and "Flowers of the Season" (#1454 G) with its flower seller, flower cart with umbrella, and bunches of gorgeous Lladró flowerwork, first issued in 1983 but, despite its considerable expense, still being produced today. Perhaps his most technically demanding tableau was the 500-piece limited-edition "Garden Party" (#1578 G), with its southern belles and five slender garden arches that had to be held up in the kiln with special arch supports. Puche was also the principal sculptor for the Zaphir brand (*illus. p. 111*).

ANTONIO RAMOS

Lladró's miniaturist, producing the series of animal miniatures from the 1980s (#s 5308–5318 G and #s 5432–5438 G, *illus. p. 66*). Revels in minute detail and enjoys working in tight spaces even on larger pieces (*illus. p. 50*). Sculpted the delightful Gres sultans (#2338–2339) and the fantastic Gres saxophonist model "Playing the Blues" (#3576). His contribution to Lladró's Black Legacy line was a series of three "Jazz Band" models (#s 5928–5930 G). Designed the wonderful grouping of several boys playing with their puppies in the park, "Puppy Dog Tails" (#5339 G). Also sculpted Lladró's Klimt Collection, noted for its decorative detail, including "The Kiss" (#1921), a limited edition of only eighty pieces retired in 2008.

JOSÉ RAUSSELL

This name appears only a couple of times in the very early history of Lladró production, associated with one model: "Sea Shell" (#0089.06 G) and "Sea Shell White" (#0215.18 G).

JOSÉ ROIG

Perhaps his most endearing model for the regular Lladró collection was "Boy with Snails" (#4896 G/M), featuring a very young child with little ding-toed feet enthralled with the snail crawling on the back of his hand. Among Roig's most well-known regular Lladró brand creations are the Sports Billy and Sports Lilly puppet figures (#s 5134–5138 G). He contributed several models to Lladró's Black Legacy line of African American themes (#s 5157–5160 G). He also designed the first complex limited-edition grouping of Cinderella and her coach in "At the Stroke of Twelve" (#1493 G). Roig produced several of the cat models in the NAO brand, including the two kittens with yarn balls (#s 257 and 259 G/M), "Collared" (#490 G/M) and "All Decked Out" (#492 G/M), and the incomparably regal "Proud Cat" (#254 G/M) (*all illus. p. 103–104*), as well as two wonderful puppy groupings (*illus. p. 95*), among other NAO models.

ALFREDO RUIZ

Alfredo Ruiz's favorite figurine theme seems to have been Papillon dogs. He produced Lladró's popular "Papillon Dog" (#4857 G/M), an early model produced for only a short time, 1974–79, and a Gres bust of a girl with Papillon (#2013). His work is, however, more frequently associated with Lladró's nonfigural items such as vases and lamps.

ANTONIO RUIZ (NAO SCULPTOR)

Antonio Ruiz's name appears sporadically in production records as an early sculptor for the NAO brand (e.g., "Shepherd on Stile" #177 G/M, "Elephant" #106 G/M, *illus. p. 106*).

ENRIQUE SAN ISIDRO

An independent artist not part of the regular Lladró stable of sculptors, San Isidro worked exclusively on the inimitable Goyescas sculptures (*illus. p. 28*) and an amazing limited edition titled "Spirit of America" (#2245) commemorating the 500th Anniversary of Columbus's discovery of America.

MIGUEL ANGEL SANTAEULALIA

A relatively new addition to Lladró's stable of sculptors, with a few models in 1995 and '96 and then progressively more in the ensuing years, Miguel Santaeulalia's most distinctive work is the Cantata series of several male and female angels (#s 8178–8183 G/M), whose distinguishing characteristic is their stylized, relief-sculpted robes. These were first issued in 2005, and all were retired in 2008 except for one glazed version (#8182) that was open until 2010. Santaeulalia also sculpts for the NAO brand (*illus. p. 97*). (See José Santaeulalia in the list of newest sculptors below, to whom Miguel may be related.)

PABLO SERRANO

Another independent artist, Serrano produced a number of highly stylized sculptures for Lladró of Don Quixote, Sancho Panza, Miguel de Cervantes, and Isabel la Católica. He also produced an owl model, which, along with the Quixote models, was done as a study series in copies of different colors.

REGINO TORRIJOS

Torrijos is a relative newcomer to the Lladró stable. His work tends to favor kids interacting with animals, as in "Meal Time" (a little girl pouring milk for kittens; #6109 G), "Birthday Party" (a little girl sharing a cake with her kittens; #6134 G), and "Down You Go" (a little girl sending a bunch of puppies down a small waterslide; #6002 G). He liked working in Gres, as in "Wake Up Kitty" (#2187, *illus. p. 79*) and "Jealous Friend" (#2108, *illus. p. 77*). Perhaps his most spectacular creation for Lladró was "Feathered Fantasy" (#5851 G), retired in 1996, featuring a showgirl with a massive "tail" of peacock feathers.

CIPRIANO VICENTE (NAO SCULPTOR)

Name appears sporadically in record of NAO sculptors.

PART II:
RECENT ADDITIONS TO THE ROSTER OF LLADRÓ SCULPTORS

As the famous early sculptors for the Lladró company age, their production naturally slows down, and, for the most part, their names now only occasionally appear as the sculptors of record for new issues. Of those listed above, several are well on in years, and at least one (Fulgencio García) is deceased. Joan Coderch, Francisco Polope, and Miguel Angel Santaeulalia, who were new to the company in the 1990s, remain very active, and their work just gets better and better! But for the most part, the famous "old guard" sculptors listed above have given way to the "new guard" listed below. While I can tell you that some beautiful new models are being produced, the sculptors listed are quite recent additions to the Lladró stable, and it would be premature, as of this writing, to attempt to characterize their work. Consequently, I have simply listed their names below without annotation. Those marked with an asterisk (*) sculpt both for Lladró's core brand *and* its NAO brand.

*Juan Ignacio Aliena**	(*illus. p. 64*)
Miguel Cruz	
Eva Maria Cuerva	(NAO sculptor)
Francisco Cuesta	
Virginia González	
*Juan Carlos Ferri Herrero**	(*illus. p. 65*)
Alfredo Llorens	(*illus. p. 74*)
Rafael Lozano	(NAO sculptor)
*José Javier Malavia**	(*illus. p. 73*)
*Ernest Massuet**	(*illus. p. 146*)
Javier Molina	
*Marco Antonio Noguerón**	
*Raul Rubio**	
*José Santaeulalia**	(*illus. pp. 45, 97*)
Javier Santes	(NAO sculptor)
*José Luis Santes**	(*illus. pp. 135, 140*)

NOTES

INTRODUCTION

1. For US collectors looking for replacement value for insuring their collections, one of the best sources for replacement value on regular-collection Lladró is Janet Hammer's website, A Retired Collection (www.ARetiredCollection.com). (She does not deal in Lladró's alternate brands such as NAO and Zaphir.) This company has a wide-ranging network of contacts in the Lladró world, and, because it is often the only practical source at all for acquiring rare items, most insurance companies accept its prices as replacement values.

CHAPTER 1

1. José Lladró, *Passenger of Life; Memories and Opinions of an Entrepreneur* (Barcelona: Editorial Planeta, 2002), 48.
2. Ibid., 53.
3. Ibid., 121–124.
4. Ibid., 53.
5. "Rights of Passage," *Expressions* 1, no. 2 (Summer 1985).
6. Special Events column, *Expressions* 6, no. 2 (Summer 1990): 11.
7. "The Favorite Figurine of José Lladró, 'Sad Harlequin,'" *Expressions* 13, no. 1 (1997): 4. (*Expressions* was the magazine of the now-defunct Lladró Collectors Society.)
8. Robert Schmidt, *Porcelain as an Art and a Mirror of Fashion* (London: George G. Harrad, 1932), 186.
9. "Tracking the Arrival of All Aboard," *Expressions* 8, no. 1 (Spring 1992): 5.
10. For a fascinating account of this mammoth undertaking, see "The 18th Century Coach," *Expressions* 4, no. 1 (Spring 1988): 19–23.
11. "Trial by Fire," *Expressions* 12, no. 1 (Spring 1996): 11.
12. Roger J. Heritage, *Royal Copenhagen Porcelain Animals and Figurines* (Atglen, PA: Schiffer, 1997), 6.
13. Schmidt, *Porcelain as an Art and a Mirror of Fashion*, 256; and John Sanborn, *Miller's Collecting Porcelain* (London: Octopus, 2002), 91.
14. Ricard Ramon Camps, "Industria, cultura popular, y estéticas de la innocencia; Disney, Lladró, y las Fallas de Valencia," *Millars* 38, no. 9 (2015): 197–222.

CHAPTER 2

1. US Court of Appeals, 9th Circuit, *Diseños Artísticos e Industriales, S.A.; Lladró USA, Inc.; Plaintiffs-Appellees, v. Costco Wholesale Corporation, Defendant-Appellant*, 97 F.3d 377. Decided October 8, 1996.
2. "Lladró [1989–90] Festival and Auction Information," *A Work of Art* 2, no. 1 (Winter 1991): 6–11.
3. "Lladró 1995 Florida Auction Prices with Comparative 1994 California and 1994 Florida Auction Prices," *A Work of Art*, Spring 1995.
4. "Lladró 1995 California Prices with Comparative 1994 Florida and 1994 California Auction Prices," *A Work of Art*, Winter 1995–96, 6–10. (I have not included the volume and number on this and the previous source citation because the publisher has inadvertently duplicated the numbers; therefore, we should rely on issue dates for the distinction between the issues.)
5. See chapter 7 for Vicente Lladró's observations on this point.

CHAPTER 3
---

1. José Lladró, *Passenger of Life*, 99.
2. "History," NAO Porcelain, www.naoporcelain.com/nao/porcelana/historia/.
3. "NAO Made in Spain," NAO Porcelain, www.naoporcelain.com/nao/porcelana/confeccion. It is quite possible, given the sketchy record of company brand chronology, that NAO began even earlier than 1968.
4. José Lladró, *Passenger of Life*, 84.
5. *NAO, Hand Made in Spain by Lladró Edición, 1987–88* (Tavernes Blanques, Spain). Manufacturer retail catalog.
6. "A Quiz for NAO," *Expressions* 1, no. 4 (1985): 4–5.

CHAPTER 4
---

1. José Lladró, *Passenger of Life*, 98.
2. Ibid., 99.

CHAPTER 5
---

1. Rosal was also an invented Lladró brand, but, as we'll see in the next chapter, its purpose was not intentional brand diversification.
2. *Golden Memories Retail Catalog for 1994* (Tavernes Blanques, Spain: Fernando Gil, 1994).

CHAPTER 6
---

1. José Lladró, *Passenger of Life*, 95–99.
2. Ibid., 87.
3. Ibid., 96.
4. José Lladró, *Passenger of Life*, 53.

CHAPTER 7

1. My English translation of a phrase in Eugenio Mallol, "Lladró saca lustre a sus 'Best Sellers,'" *El Mundo*, June 1, 2009, col. 6, p. 13.

2. Ibid. Also Joaquim Clemente Valencia, "Lladró despide a 275 empleados al agravarse su situación por la crisis," *Cinco Dias*, October 17, 2008, Empresas [business section], 13.

3. "Love II Couple Figurine," official Lladró website, accessed July 22, 2018, www.lladro.com/en_us/love-ii-couple-figurine.html.

4. "Lladró, la empresa familiar que cambia de manos," *Infocif, la Red Socialde Empresas*, http://noticias.infocif.es/noticia/una-empresa-conocida-tambien-por-las-malas-relaciones-familiares.

5. Inés Herrero, "Vicente Lladró aprueba la propuesta de PHI Industrial pero no asistirá a la votación," *Economía: Las Provincias*, December 10, 2016, www.lasprovincias.es/economia/201612/10/vicente-lladro-aprueba-propuesta-20161210001927-v.html.

6. Inés Herrero, "Temo que la empresa Lladró, en breve, no sea de la familia ni de los valencianos," *Economía: Las Provincias*, October 25, 2016, www.lasprovincias.es/economia/201610/25/temo-empresa-lladro-breve-20161024234857.html.

7. Herrero, "Vicente Lladró aprueba la propuesta de PHI Industrial pero no asistirá a la Votación."

8. José Luis Zaragozá, "El fondo PHI mantendrá la marca Lladró y garantiza el empleo en 2017," *Levante: El Mercantil Valenciano*, January 17, 2017.

9. Luis A. Torralba, "Quién es PHI Industrial, futuro propietario de Lladró?" *ValenciaPlaza.com*, http://valenciaplaza.com/quien-es-phi-industrial-futuro-propietario-de-lladro.

10. Herrero, "Temo que la empresa Lladró, en breve, no sea de la familia ni de los valencianos."

11. "Lladró tuvo casi todos los problemas típicos de empresa familiar, según un experto," *EFE Valencia*, January 20, 2017, www.efe.com/efe/comunitat-valenciana/economia/lladro-tuvo-casi-todos-los-problemas-tipicos-de-empresa-familiar-segun-un-experto/50000882-3154738.

BIBLIOGRAPHY

"The 18th Century Coach." *Expressions* 4, no. 1 (Spring 1988): 19–23.

Camps, Ricard Ramon. "Industria, cultura popular, y estéticas de la innocencia; Disney, Lladró, y las Fallas de Valencia." *Millars* 38, no. 9 (2015).

Cerámicas Hispania Catalogo [retail catalog]. Tavernes Blanques, Spain: Fernando Gil, 1984.

"The Favorite Figurine of José Lladró, 'Sad Harlequin.'" *Expressions* 13, no. 1 (1997).

Golden Memories Retail Catalog for 1994. Tavernes Blanques, Spain: Fernando Gil, 1994.

Heritage, Roger J. *Royal Copenhagen Porcelain Animals and Figurines*. Atglen, PA: Schiffer, 1997.

Herrero, Inés. "Temo que la empresa Lladró, en breve, no sea de la familia ni de los valencianos." *Economía: Las Provincias*, October 25, 2016. www.lasprovincias.es/economia/201610/25/temo-empresa-lladro-breve-20161024234857.html (accessed January 31, 2017).

———. "Vicente Lladró aprueba la propuesta de PHI Industrial pero no asistirá a la votación." *Economía: Las Provincias*, December 10, 2016. www.lasprovincias.es/economia/201612/10/vicente-lladro-aprueba-propuesta-20161210001927-v.html (accessed January 31, 2017).

Lladró. *Lladró: The Art of Porcelain; How Spanish Porcelain Became World Famous*. Barcelona: Salvat Editores, 1981.

Lladró. *Lladró: The Magic World of Porcelain*. Barcelona: Salvat Editores, 1989.

Lladró. *Lladró: The Will to Create*. Tavernes Blanques, Spain: Fernando Gil, 1998.

The Lladró Encyclopedia. 4 vols. Tavernes Blanques, Spain: Sociedad de Coleccionistas Lladró / Lladró Collectors Society, n.d. (but covering issues from earliest days through 1994).

"Lladró [1989–90] Festival and Auction Information." *A Work of Art* 2, no. 1 (Winter 1991): 6–11.

Lladró, José. *Passenger of Life: Memoirs and Opinions of an Entrepreneur*. Barcelona: Editorial Planeta, 2002.

"Lladró, la empresa familiar que cambia de manos." *Infocif, la Red Socialde Empresas*. http://noticias.infocif.es/noticia/una-empresa-conocida-tambien-por-las-malas-relaciones-familiares (accessed January 31, 2017).

"Lladró 1995 California Auction Prices with Comparative 1994 Florida and 1994 California Auction Prices." *A Work of Art*, Winter 1995–96, 6–10.

"Lladró 1995 Florida Auction Prices with Comparative 1994 California and Florida Auction Prices." *A Work of Art*, Spring 1995, 4–7.

Lladró Porcelain [official Lladró website]. www.lladro.com.

Lladró Porcelain (retail catalog). Galway, Ireland: Stephen Faller, 1971.

"Lladró tuvo casi todos los problemas típicos de empresa familiar, según un experto." *EFE Valencia*, January 20, 2017. www.efe.com/efe/comunitat-valenciana/economia/lladro-tuvo-casi-todos-los-problemas-tipicos-de-empresa-familiar-segun-un-experto/50000882-3154738 (accessed January 31, 2017).

Lladró USA. *The Lladró Authorized Reference Guide*. Moonachie, NJ: Lladró USA, 2006.

Mallol, Eugenio. "Lladró saca lustre a sus 'Best Sellers.'" *El Mundo*, June 1, 2009.

NAO, Hand Made in Spain by Lladró Edición, 1987-88 [retail catalog]. Tavernes Blanques, Spain.

NAO Porcelain [official NAO website]. www.naoporcelain.com.

El Portal Porcelana [website for identifying Lladró brands]. www.elportalporcelana.info.

"A Quiz for NAO." *Expressions* 1, no. 4 (Winter 1985).

A Retired Collection [broker of retired Lladró]. www.aRetiredCollection.com.

"Rights of Passage." *Expressions* 1, no. 2 (Summer 1985).

Sanborn, John. *Miller's Collecting Porcelain*. London: Octopus, 2002.

Schmidt, Robert. *Porcelain as an Art and a Mirror of Fashion*. London: George G. Harrad, 1932.

Special Events column, *Expressions* 6, no. 2 (Summer 1990).

Torralba, Luis A. "Quién es PHI Industrial, futuro propietario de Lladró?" *ValenciaPlaza.com*, http://valenciaplaza.com/quien-es-phi-industrial-futuro-propietario-de-lladro (accessed January 31, 2017).

"Tracking the Arrival of All Aboard." *Expressions* 8, no. 1 (Spring 1992).

"Trial by Fire." *Expressions* 12, no. 1 (Spring 1996).

US Court of Appeals, 9th Circuit. *Diseños Artísticos e Industriales, S.A.; Lladró USA, Inc.; Plaintiffs-Appellees v. Costco Wholesale Corporation, Defendant-Appellant*. 97 F.3d 377. Decided October 8, 1996.

Valencia, Joachim Clemente. "Lladró despide a 275 empleados al agravarse su situación por la crisis." *Cinco Dias*, October 17, 2008.

Zaphir: Arte y Porcelanas, SA [1978 retail catalog]. Paterna, Spain: Artes Gráficas Vicent, 1978.

Zaragozá, José Luis. "El fondo PHI mantendrá la marca Lladró y garantiza el empleo en 2017." *Levante: El Mercantil Valenciano*, January 17, 2017.

INDEX

Particular models in this index are arranged alphabetically within their respective brand headings, with the brand sections arranged according to the chronology of their production.

LLADRÓ CORE COLLECTION MODELS

NAO

ZAPHIR

GOLDEN MEMORIES

OTHER LLADRÓ AND LLADRÓ-AFFILIATED BRANDS (ROSAL, TANG, HISPANIA)

ABOUT THE AUTHOR

Peggy Rose Whiteneck is known for her research into the growth of the Lladró secondary-collector market. Her website on Spanish porcelain has an international following, and she is frequently contacted for Lladró answers by collectors and secondary-market dealers from around the world. She writes feature articles on antiques and collectibles, including a national syndicated column titled "Good Eye: A Collector's View of the Antiques and Collectibles Trade."

The URL for her website on Spanish porcelain is
WWW.ELPORTALPORCELANA.INFO